visit *slatterymedia.com*

The Slattery Media Group
1 Albert Street, Richmond
Victoria, Australia, 3121
visit slatterymedia.com

Text copyright © Victoria Heywood, 2012
Illustrations copyright © Bill Wood, 2012
First published by the The Slattery Media Group, 2012

All rights reserved. No part of this publication may be reproduced, stored in a retrieval system or transmitted in any form by any means without the prior permission of the copyright owner. Inquiries should be made to the publisher.

National Library of Australia Cataloguing-in-Publication entry

Title: Good cook bad cook / Victoria Heywood ; edited by Helen Alexander ; illustrated by Bill Wood.
Author: Heywood, Victoria.
ISBN: 9781921778544 (pbk.)
Subjects: Cooking.
Other Authors/Contributors: Alexwood, Helen. Wood, Bill, 1966-
Dewey Number: 641.5

Group Publisher: Geoff Slattery
Author: Victoria Heywood
Editor: Helen Alexander
Creative Director: Guy Shield
Designer: Kate Slattery
Illustrations: Bill Wood

Printed in China through APOL

DEDICATION

For my son, Jerome,
may he learn to cook well,
and in memory of
my father, Stewart Heywood
(1925-2004), who did.

GOOD COOK ★ BAD COOK

CONTENTS

INTRODUCTION	**6**
20 RULES FOR KITCHEN NOVICES	**9**
BREAKFAST	**12**
★ Scrambled eggs	14
★ Hotcakes	16
★ Omelette	18
★ Hash browns	20
★ Baked beans	22
★ Pancakes	24
★ Poached eggs	26
★ Breakfast bars	28
★ Muffins	30
SNACKS	**32**
★ Croque monsieur	34
★ Croquettes	36
★ Sandwiches	38
★ Pizza	40
★ Quiche	42
★ Chicken nuggets	44
SOUPS	**46**
★ Gazpacho	48
★ Tomato soup	50
★ Minestrone	52
★ Pumpkin soup	54
★ French onion soup	56
VEGETABLES	**58**
★ Asparagus	60
★ Eggplant	62
★ Roast and mashed potatoes	64
★ Chips	66
★ Avocado	68
★ Zucchini	70
★ Vegetable salad	72
PASTA AND NOODLES	**74**
★ Homemade pasta	76
★ Shop-bought pasta	78
★ Bolognese	80
★ Gnocchi	82
★ Macaroni cheese	84

RICE AND GRAINS — 86
- Risotto — 88
- Couscous — 90
- Tabouli — 92
- Quinoa — 94

FISH AND SHELLFISH — 96
- Fish en papillote — 98
- Salmon — 100
- Fish pie — 102
- Squid — 104
- Moules marinières — 106
- Tempura prawns — 108

MEATS — 110
- Steak — 112
- Roast chicken — 114
- Beef casserole — 116
- Hamburger — 118
- Sausages — 120
- Pork stir-fry — 122
- Roast pork — 124
- Roast lamb — 126

SAUCES AND CONDIMENTS · 128
- Béchamel sauce — 130
- Hollandaise sauce — 132
- Vinaigrette — 134
- Pesto — 136
- Tapenade — 138
- Mayonnaise — 140
- Jam — 142
- Custard — 144

DESSERTS AND BAKING — 146
- Shortcrust pastry — 148
- Lemon tart — 150
- Trifle — 152
- Sponge — 154
- Apple pie — 156
- Fruit crumble — 158
- Peach melba — 160
- Scones — 162
- Berry tart — 164
- Biscuits — 166
- Ice cream — 168
- Brownies — 170
- Cupcakes — 172
- Meringues — 174
- Pavlova — 176
- Chocolate fudge cake — 178
- Bread — 180

DRINKS — 182
- Hot chocolate — 184
- Smoothie — 186
- Lemonade — 188
- Iced tea — 190
- Champagne punch — 192

GOOD COOK ★ BAD COOK

INTRODUCTION

This is a book of fundamentals—the dishes that we all love and eat regularly. Cooking isn't rocket science. It's about fine ingredients, treated with respect and an understanding as to what works and why.

The dry risotto. The gluggy pasta. The leaden scones that no amount of cream can save. The roast chicken that's promisingly golden on the outside and running with blood within. The execrable takeaway re-warmed in the microwave. The veggie stir-fry that's cooked to mush.

There's no doubt that the average kitchen today sees more crimes against humanity than the International Court of Justice handles in a year.

And yes, good food may be a first-world problem, but it's an important one. Good food is soul food—bad food leads to crankiness, constipation and spots, and is doubtless the driving force behind today's obesity epidemic. Eat good food, and you'll be sitting around the table grinning contentedly; eat bad food and you'll be looking for some extra carby comfort before you know it.

We live in a privileged society, with great ingredients at our fingertips, running water at the end of a tap, and gas or electricity at the flick of a switch. So why do we accept less than the best? Why do we eat tepid take out while watching gastroporn cooking shows? Why spend a fortune at the butcher's only to butcher the end result? Hell, if a 15th-century Italian peasant could throw together a perfectly good meal from a bunch of basil, some garlic, parmesan and pasta after a long day toiling in the fields, then surely we can do the same after a day at the office? We need to man up in the kitchen—men and women alike.

Cooking isn't rocket science. It's about fine ingredients, treated with respect and a smidgeon of understanding as to what works and why.

So this book is written for all those who want to cook good food rather than the alternative. It's for those who are starting out in the kitchen, who don't want to poison or embarrass themselves or others. It's for those otherwise competent folk who remain flummoxed by certain dishes while being perfectly capable of acing others. Trust me, it's possible for anyone to cook feather-light scones or deliver up beautifully cooked fish with a sauce that sings. This book is also for those who want to perfect some classics, and understand how the hell we got here in the first place.

This is a book of fundamentals—the dishes that we all love and eat regularly. You'll find no foams here, or tricky restaurant fare, just good food that will give you a lifetime of happy eating.

INTRODUCTION

This book should be in the backpack of every person leaving their mother's apron strings—*and* in the Christmas stocking of every kid still living at home and old enough to rustle up their own dinners once in a while.

But first, let's get one thing straight: good food comes from good cooks, and good cooks aren't born—they're made. Even super-chefs like Heston Blumenthal and Nigel Slater and Stephanie Alexander didn't come kicking and screaming from the womb, shouting: "I've a great idea for bacon and egg ice cream!" or "I know how to cook the perfect leg of lamb. With anchovies!" First you need to master the basics, and only then should you be free to experiment.

Far from many cooks spoiling the broth, all it takes is one over-confident kitchen klutz who cooks with good intentions, but no clue. The kind of cook who thinks that sushi is nice, burritos are nice—hey, how about a sushi burrito?! The same thought process is likely responsible for similar monsters such as curried pizza, coriander pesto, banana guacamole, marshmallow coleslaw and other travesties.

And don't even get me started on the perils of meals in cardboard boxes or 'just add water' powdered mixes. Forget fusion food—our world is being taken over by frankenfood, packed with chemicals, genetically modified ingredients and all sorts of other nasties.

It's time we got back to basics, starting with great ingredients in season, not flown thousands of miles and yanked from the cool room of the supermarket. And the basics of technique, too.

Think about the classics, like bangers and mash, lasagne, roast chicken, chocolate cake, apple pie… In the hands of a cook who knows what they're doing, these trusty dishes always seem to turn out just right. And the reason why? The cook has made them so often that every little wrinkle in the process has been ironed out.

Sure, occasionally the cook tinkers around the edges a bit—perhaps to suit the needs of an unfamiliar oven, or to account for a sudden change in available ingredients, but essentially the recipe, the process and the whole look and feel of the dish as it's coming together are imprinted into the good cook's DNA. Think of how your grandmother could pull off a perfect Sunday roast. She could probably manage it after half a bottle of sherry. (And probably did, if my family is any indication.)

I grew up in the 70s, so the kinds of dishes my father could turn out without fail included Sunday night curried eggs (béchamel sauce flavoured with curry powder, with the cunning addition of mashed boiled eggs, served on hot buttered toast) and a lethal cocktail called 'Norwegian tiger's milk', which saw many dinner party guests staggering home to bed before dinner was even served. A shame, really, as it often included another of Dad's trusted favourites—Tasmanian scallops lightly pan-fried in lemon, butter, garlic and parsley.

All of these recipes had something in common. They celebrated simple ingredients cooked well, and were designed for a very specific purpose, respectively: 1) comfort food for family, and 2) the joy of entertaining friends. Once Dad was onto a good thing, he stuck to it. He cooked and cooked and cooked and cooked, until he could cook the damn dish in his sleep. I suggest you do the same with the recipes here. Make them part of your DNA, too.

For me, these days, curried eggs don't really cut the mustard. But I have to say that the lemon scallops are still on the menu.

Unlike many recipe books, in this one I've tried to distil all the knowledge you need to make the dish turn out perfectly. You know, the kind of tips and tricks your grandmother picked up at the knee of her grandmother. To broaden my understanding of what works and why, I also immersed myself in some hefty reference tomes: Harold McGee's *On Food and Cooking: The Science and Lore of the Kitchen*; Michael Ruhlman's *The Elements of Cooking*, and of course, *Larousse Gastronomique*, aptly subtitled 'the world's greatest cookery encyclopaedia'. Mashed together with information from all sorts of other sources, all tested in my kitchen at home, I like to think that this book doesn't just give you recipes for 80 classic dishes, but also clear guidance on how not to stuff them up. In one day alone, I made eight, yes EIGHT, different pavlovas, testing to see what happened when I changed the balance of the ingredients and ignored long-standing kitchen lore. Answer: disaster. There's a reason why you should stick to a good recipe when you find it.

This book is organised into the usual suspects—breakfast, baking, meats, vegetables, and so on—but within this, you'll find lots of useful links. For example, once you've mastered the art of a good béchamel sauce, a squillion other dishes are now at your fingertips—cauliflower cheese, macaroni and cheese and fish pie, to name but a few. The same for basics such as a buttery shortcrust pastry, which can be transformed into the base for pies, both savoury and sweet. Also a speedy hollandaise, which can be lavished over fish, asparagus, eggs, smoked salmon, ham or whatever else takes your fancy. There are also links between techniques—once you've got the hang of whipping egg whites for a meringue, suddenly pavlova, soufflé, and more are all within your reach. And that perfect custard of yours? Enjoy it as is, or turn it into a trifle or an ice cream.

So with endless permutations and combinations—just some of which I've noted here—this book is the basis for literally hundreds of meals, snacks and other tasty treats. Enjoy.

One final word of warning: yes, it's great to be able to cook good food at home, but t here is one side effect you should be aware of: restaurant rage. Next thing you know, you'll be down the pub or at your local Italian ordering a veal parma and you'll find yourself looking at the sauce-slathered slab on your plate thinking: "It's just a frozen, pre-shaped schnitzel, tossed straight from the freezer into the deep-fryer, and covered in commercial sauce. Hell, I can do better than that."

Congratulations. You now know the difference between good food and bad.

Victoria Heywood, October 2012

GOOD COOK ✶ BAD COOK

20 RULES FOR KITCHEN NOVICES

1. Good food starts with good ingredients. Find a decent butcher, fishmonger and greengrocer—you never know when you'll need them to pin bone a side of salmon, or save you some offaly good bits that aren't generally available. And hunt down a good supply of quality fresh and dried pasta, as well as rice, oils, cheese and spices.

Supermarkets are good for loo paper, but not always great for world-class produce, lovingly selected and prepared by experts who, like some mothers at playgroup, will bend your ear about their offspring's home environment, developmental progress and all-round superiority.

2. Never drive past a farmers' market. Stallholders actively encourage you to eat as you shop, which is generally frowned upon in supermarkets, plus you never know what you might find in season.

3. Eat seasonally and locally. That's why farmers' markets are so good. You're unlikely to find some Chinese garlic grower has flown halfway around the world to set up shop, but he may well have sent his bulbs as unaccompanied baggage to a shop near you.

It's not just about the air miles—although you should care about those, too—it's also about the amount of time those bulbs might have spent in detention in a warehouse somewhere. Food grown locally is likely to be fresher, less tired and certainly less homesick.

4. Keep your pantry well stocked and you'll always be able to throw together a quick meal. A full-to-bursting cupboard saves time and provides the basis for many good meals.

5. There's no substitute for good salt (not the iodised powder) and freshly ground black pepper. Pre-ground pepper is a bit like sprinkling flea dirt over your meal.

6. Never use cheap fats. There are basically three food groups involved in cooking: protein, carbohydrates and fats. And it doesn't matter how good your protein and carbs might be—if you cover them in low-quality olive oil or cheap margarine, then the end result will be low-quality and cheap.

Great olive oil can make the plainest of dishes sing, and butter is just simply better in nine out of 10 cases.

7. If you can read, you can cook. No excuses. Read through the recipe first, and make sure you have all the ingredients before you start. Also the necessary kit. There's nothing worse than getting to the end of a recipe to find, dang it, that you need some special kind of tin for baking your cake.

8. Measure out everything before you start. There's a reason why TV chefs have those dinky containers of pre-prepared ingredients—well, several really. First, it makes them look like a TV chef, which is kind of essential when you are a TV chef. Second, it's a way of double-checking that you have everything you need. And third, it saves time during the process so you're not constantly interrupting the flow to chop parsley, reduce stock, weigh flour…

9. Don't freak out about kitchen gear. All you really need to get started is a knife, a spoon, a bowl and a few pots and pans of some sort. Anything else is a bonus—from killer sharp knives to Le Crueset. Plus, too many gadgets can kill creativity. How often have you really used that doughnut maker you bought on sale?

Buy good stuff that's going to last and become part of the family—not cheap rubbish that makes an appearance once every decade, a bit like that dodgy third cousin of yours.

10. Use a bigger mixing bowl than you think you need. Ever seen someone try to toss a Caesar salad for four in a cereal bowl? Start with a big bowl, straight up, and you'll avoid making a mess and dirtying more dishes than you need.

11. Keep tasting. Don't wait till the end of the cooking time or allow your dinner guests to discover for themselves that you forgot to add any salt or that an egg was past its best.

Taste and season every step of the way. Taste when you add a new ingredient, and then taste again just before you serve. You'll not only learn how the flavours change and meld throughout the process, but you'll be serving up something that's really good.

12. Looks matter. It's incredible what happens when you arrange cooked food on a nice piece of china rather than dolloping it onto a scratched plastic picnic plate. Same food, a very different eating experience. The eyes are the windows to the stomach, or however the saying goes, so put some effort into the finishing touches.

20 RULES FOR KITCHEN NOVICES

13. Stay safe. Cooking is fun, but there are lots of things that can go wrong, too: sharp knives, fire hazards, cross-contamination, slippery banana skins and the rest. Remember to use your common sense.

14. Clean as you go. That way you run less risk of: 1) divorce, and 2) losing a small child or lovingly prepared dish among all the dirty plates and pots.

15. Don't be afraid of screwing up. Disasters can and do happen—to everyone, no exceptions. For that reason alone, it's best to steer clear of tricky new recipes when entertaining and opt for foolproof favourites that you can throw together without a thought, even with a few convivial glasses of wine under your belt.

16. Eat out as often as your wallet and waistline will allow. Try new restaurants, new cuisines, or even new dishes from a familiar menu. People who love food and are endlessly curious about tastes, textures and combinations make the best cooks.

If you've always been too intimidated to cook tofu or asparagus or whole fish, then eat it as much as you can, prepared by professionals, first. That way, you get to know what it's meant to look and taste like before you try doing it yourself.

17. Don't get cocky. Improvising before you really know how to cook is a recipe for disaster. That's why Heston Blumenthal is a legend, and the rest of us are not. It takes courage, imagination, lots of experience and knowledge to come up with a dish like snail porridge or cheese on toast ice cream that's actually edible.

18. Have one great recipe that you are happy with, but not content. Keep testing, varying and improving it. This is the best way to learn how to get the best from your new cookery skills.

19. Keep learning and don't turn into an annoying foodie know-it-all. It's one thing to understand the difference between good and bad food, and how to cook the former, it's a completely different matter to bore everyone rigid with your views.

20. Relax. Not even the experts agree on the perfect way to cook certain dishes. But you can cook, and you can cook well, as long as you relax, do it with pleasure and confidence and, ideally, a glass of good wine. The food will be better for it. You certainly will be.

BREAKFAST

SCRAMBLED EGGS 14
HOTCAKES 16
OMELETTE 18
HASH BROWNS 20
BAKED BEANS 22
PANCAKES 24
POACHED EGGS 26
BREAKFAST BARS 28
MUFFINS 30

CHAPTER 1
BREAKFAST

There's something immensely satisfying about cooking breakfast, rather than just pouring cereal and milk into a bowl. For a start, anything you actually make yourself has to be more interesting. For seconds, being able to whip up a brilliantly cooked breakfast immediately sets you apart from toddlers, teenagers and 95 per cent of the rest of the population.

Best of all, many breakfast-brunch favourites—poached eggs, omelettes, and the like—can serve double duty for lunch, in-between-meal snacking, or even a light dinner at a pinch. So that's why they call it an all-day breakfast...

SCRAMBLED EGGS

You can just imagine the delight of the first hungry person who smashed his eggs on the way back to the cave, decided to cook them anyway, and ended up inventing scrambled eggs. Written references to this dish date back to Roman times, only popping up in English cuisine in the 16th century, where they were also known as buttered or jumbled eggs.

Although today they're considered a 'basic' dish, making scrambled eggs takes practice. And it requires constant attention—you can't walk away and leave them to their own devices.

Make sure the pan is heated and the butter foamy (but not browned) before you add the eggs. Think low and slow—too much heat will cook the eggs too quickly, leaving pockets of goo inside the layers of cooked egg. Likewise, too much vigorous stirring will dry the eggs out and make them powdery. And on no account should you ever cook them so much that they start to brown! What you're looking to create are light, fluffy, golden curds that are soft and creamy—not rubbery or dry.

SERVES 1

Ingredients

2 free-range eggs

1 tablespoon water, full-cream milk or cream

salt and black pepper

20g butter

buttered toast, to serve

Optional additions include
a handful of chopped fresh herbs, grated cheese or slivers of ham

Method

1. Crack the eggs into a medium-sized bowl and remove any blood spots or bits of shell. Add the milk or cream (or water for a fluffier result) and use a fork to lightly whisk until just combined. Don't overbeat the eggs. Season to taste.

2. Melt the butter in a saucepan over medium heat. Swirl the pan around so the butter coats the base.

3. When the butter is just starting to foam, pour in the egg mix. Let it cook for 30 seconds, then use a wooden spoon to stir gently and continuously until the egg mixture starts forming creamy curds. Push the formed curds towards the centre and tilt the pan so the runny bits flow to the edge. Break apart any large pieces as they form with your spoon—you want fluffy little pillows, not great big beanbags.

4. When the eggs have reached the point where they show just a tiny bit of moisture on the surface (around 2-3 minutes), add any additional ingredients, such as cheese or herbs, and remove from the heat. Stir once more and serve on slices of buttered toast.

5. When eaten for breakfast, scrambled eggs are often dished up alongside hash browns, bacon or sausages. You can also spice them up with any number of sauces—tomato, HP, chilli or Worcestershire.

TIPS FOR PERFECTION

* Use a spatula or wooden spoon. A whisk will break up the eggs too much and powdery little yellow crumbs will be created.
* The lower the heat and the more constant the movement, the creamier the end product. Stir the mix just like you would a soup, making sure to keep all the curds moving so they don't stick to the bottom or sides of the pan and brown.
* The eggs should be slightly undercooked when you remove them from the heat. The residual heat will continue to cook them even as you slide them onto the buttered toast.

BAD SCRAMBLED EGGS

It's a truth universally acknowledged that on any long-haul flight, you'll be served scrambled eggs during at least one leg of the trip. And no matter what airline you fly, the eggy offering is always the same—rubbery but powdery at the same time, and somehow tasting of stale farts. You can achieve much the same result at home by using powdered eggs, adding water and nuking them in the microwave, but I seriously wouldn't advise it. Even if you use real eggs—the kind that come in a shell and not from a packet—and make sure to stop the machine and stir every few seconds, you'll still end up with rubber.

Going to the other foodie extreme, I also wouldn't bother with the classical technique for scrambled eggs, which involves slow cooking in a double boiler and an aching amount of slow whisking. Who has the time? A well-buttered saucepan and some steady wrist action will deliver much the same results.

HOTCAKES

Pancake or hotcake? It's all a matter of personal preference, and while some people can't get enough of the European-style thin pancake (see page 24) others opt for the puffy and stacked version made with buttermilk the American way.

These thick, spongy hotcakes can be made with all manner of grains, from fine cornmeal to a combination of plain flour and rye, buckwheat or wholemeal flour. You can also use plain milk if you don't have any buttermilk handy, and fudge the batter by souring the milk with a splash of lemon juice. But fat-free or low-fat milk is a no-no. You will just end up with a thinner, more watery reflection of the real thing.

Feel free to experiment with spices and other ingredients—replace 50g of the flour with 50g of cocoa for chocolate hotcakes, or try sprinkling cinnamon in with the flour—this version goes beautifully with stewed or caramelised apples.

For extra fluffy pancakes, substitute self-raising flour for the plain flour and use the baking powder as well. But remember the real fluffiness comes from the inclusion of softly whipped egg whites, folded gently into the batter. They are a little more time-consuming to make than the flat pancake, but the end result is nirvana for those who like them hot… cakes.

MAKES 12

Ingredients

3 eggs, separated

2 cups buttermilk (or full-cream milk soured with lemon juice)

2 tablespoons melted butter (allowed to cool slightly) or olive oil, plus extra for cooking

300g plain flour

1 teaspoon baking powder

½ teaspoon salt

2 tablespoons caster sugar

Method

1. Beat the egg yolks until light yellow and creamy, then whisk in the buttermilk and melted butter or olive oil.

2. Sift all the dry ingredients together in a bowl. Fold into the egg and buttermilk mixture. You can prepare up until this stage, then cover the batter and leave in the fridge overnight to speed things up for breakfast in the morning.

3. When you're ready to cook, whip the egg whites to soft peaks and fold into the batter. Do this gently, so as to keep the mix light and airy.

4. Lightly grease a heavy-based frying pan (cast iron is best as it helps spread the heat evenly) with the extra butter, and spoon in about ¼ cup of batter. If it's looking a bit wonky, use a spoon to spread the batter out into the shape of a circle. You can cook a few at a time if you have the room.

5. Cook each hotcake until bubbles start appearing on the top, then flip with a spatula and cook the other side.

6. Serve the hotcakes with fresh strawberries and good vanilla ice cream, or perhaps some chunky apple slices cooked in butter and brown sugar, with dollops of thick cream on top. Or use half buckwheat flour and half plain flour and serve with maple syrup and curls of crispy bacon.

SELLING LIKE...

Who would have thought that pancakes lightened with whipped egg white and cooked in bear fat or pork lard would be so popular? The Oxford English Dictionary claims that the phrase 'selling like hotcakes' first cropped up in North America in the early 19th century, when they were cooked this way. Hotcakes—often sold at church benefits and fairs and other functions—were so popular that they were soon associated with anything that sold in huge numbers, very quickly. For other toppings that will help your hotcakes sell like, well hotcakes, refer to pancakes (see page 24).

BAD HOTCAKES

To truly achieve hotcake perfection, you must make them from scratch. The packaged mixes, while useful if you're in a rush or just bone-lazy, don't come close to the taste and texture of your own homemade brew.

Luckily, there's not much you can do to screw up a hotcake, except to leave it unattended on the stove until it turns to charcoal. However, it does help to have all the ingredients at room temperature before you start. If you let hot, melted butter hit ice-cold milk, you'll get little butter globules rather than a smooth mixture.

One final tip is to avoid any recipe suggesting that peanut butter makes a fine addition to the batter. Trust me, it doesn't. Instead of hotcakes, you'll end up with peanut-flavoured coasters and not even spreading them with jam will make them edible.

BREAKFAST

OMELETTE

Even if all you have is a carton of eggs, you have the makings of a great breakfast. Cooked to golden perfection, an omelette can also do sterling service as a light lunch or supper, perhaps beefed up with some dressed salad leaves on the side and crusty bread. Ideally your omelette should be cooked in a cast-iron pan, as this helps distribute the heat perfectly. However, you can cook an omelette in practically anything—even the bottom of a wide saucepan if you're desperate. Once the omelette starts to set, don't be afraid to lift up the edges and see how it's progressing. Take a peek, tilt the pan and let any runny stuff flow from the middle out to the sides of the pan. But whatever you do, don't be tempted to give the eggs a flip to speed up the process—this is an omelette not a pancake, and flipping will dry it out too much.

While we think of the omelette as being French, its origins actually date back to ancient Persia, where beaten eggs were mixed with chopped herbs, fried until firm, then sliced into wedges in a dish known as *kookoo*. Variations on the plain omelette appear around the world—from the *tamagoyaki* of Japan (rolled omelette made with either rice vinegar, dashi soup stock, sugar or soy sauce) to Indian omelettes spiced with chilli, onion, coriander and cumin, or the Spanish *tortilla de patatas*—a thick omelette that's slow-cooked and contains sliced, sautéed potatoes and onions.

SERVES 1

Ingredients

3 large free-range eggs

salt and black pepper

50g butter, diced, or 2 teaspoons olive oil

Method

1. Break the eggs into a bowl, season, and using a balloon whisk or fork, lightly whisk together.

2. Heat an 18-20cm frying pan over medium heat. Add the butter or olive oil and cook until it begins to sizzle.

3. Add the egg mixture and tilt the pan so it covers the bottom. As the omelette begins to set, lift up the edges and tilt the pan again so that the runny stuff in the middle flows to the edge.

4. When the whole lot starts to softly set (the top should still look moist, without being runny) add any fillings and let the omelette cook a moment or so longer, to warm up the filling. Remove from the heat and get ready to serve.

5. Fold the fluffy cooked omelette in half (encasing any filling), slide onto a plate, sprinkle with more black pepper and serve immediately.

GREAT VARIATIONS

All sorts of fillings can be added to give your omelette extra flavour, but steer clear of watery vegetables or sauces, or you'll end up with a soggy mess. Any raw fillings, such as bacon or garlic, should be cooked before adding and the same goes for vegetables like asparagus or fresh peas.

The best time to add the filling is when the top of the omelette no longer moves when you tilt the pan. Add tangy cheddar, ham cooked in a spoonful of cream with a dash of Dijon mustard, diced cooked bacon or pancetta, mushrooms sautéed with a touch of garlic, roasted Roma tomatoes, fresh herbs—chives, parsley and sage all work well—smoked fish… the possibilities are endless!

For a sweet omelette, omit the salt and pepper and serve with runny honey or a little warmed jam. For an Asian-style omelette, add a teaspoon of rice wine and a few drops of sesame oil to the egg mix. Cook as per the recipe, arrange some finely sliced barbecued Chinese pork or cooked prawns on one half of the omelette, top with a few beansprouts, then fold in half. Drizzle with oyster or hoi sin sauce.

BAD OMELETTE

As simple as an omelette might be to whip up, there are still plenty of traps for young players. First, don't whisk the eggs too hard or you'll start to incorporate air into the mix, which will make your omelette tough. Second, don't under mix the eggs or you'll end up with lumps of slimy white. Finally, don't be tempted to keep cooking until the omelette is set on the top, unless you fancy eating a piece of yellow leather. Instead, cook the eggs quickly until the mix is lightly set on the bottom, but still a bit gooey on top.

Don't get me started on the egg-white omelettes so beloved of Hollywood starlets and social X-rays. These leave out the yolks to remove all traces of fat and cholesterol—in other words, the good stuff. As for fillings, far too many cooks go overboard. There's nothing wrong with a handful of grated cheese, herbs or slivers of smoked salmon, but really—sausage? Tuna and sweetcorn? Save the extra ingredients for a side dish, and enjoy a good omelette's simple perfection.

HASH BROWNS

Forget the Dukan diet—there's nothing better than carbs for a slap-up breakfast treat. Especially if it means lots of golden, crispy hash browns, sizzling and spitting straight from the pan. An American-diner staple, the naughty-but-nice fried goodies actually originated in Switzerland, where they were known as *rösti* and traditionally eaten by farmers for breakfast.

The best way to ensure your hash browns are crispy is to make sure your oil is very hot before you add the potatoes. If you drop the potato mix into tepid oil and hope for the best, the potatoes will absorb the oil and turn flabby. Also, don't overload the pan—the temperature of the oil drops as you add the raw patties and you need heat to get a crust.

Be careful too, to rinse the grated potato in several lots of water. This helps to get rid of the starch and prevents the mix from going grey. Squeezing as much moisture as you can from the grated potato also helps, as soggy ingredients make for soggy hash browns.

Big fat patties also run the risk of being crispy on the outside and raw in the middle. As a general rule, each patty should be formed from about two tablespoons of mix or less. Shape them how you like, round, square or rectangular, the choice is yours!

SERVES 4

Ingredients

6 medium potatoes

1 small onion, very finely chopped

1 tablespoon plain flour

salt

2 tablespoons fresh herbs (chives, thyme, oregano, rosemary), chopped finely

3 tablespoons vegetable oil (or goose fat if you have it—everything tastes better cooked in goose fat!)

salt and black pepper

fresh herbs, to serve

Method

1. Preheat the oven to 140°C (275°F). Peel the spuds and grate them on the big slots of a cheese grater (or use the appropriate food processor blade). Chuck the lot into a bowl of cold water, slosh around then remove, squishing out the water as you go. Repeat this a couple of times. On the last go, wrap the grated spuds in a clean tea towel and squeeze out any excess liquid. If you have one (and can be bothered) use a potato ricer to help press out the moisture.

2. Put the grated spuds in a bowl and add the onion, flour, a pinch of salt and the herbs, and mix well.

3. Heat about a tablespoon of oil in a frying pan until hot, then add a couple of tablespoons of the potato mix, shaped as you wish. Squash them a little with your spatula and fry on both sides until golden. You can probably cook about 3 or 4 at time, depending on the size of your pan, but don't overload it.

4. Pop the cooked hash browns in the oven to keep them warm and start frying the next lot. You'll probably need to add a little more oil to the pan each time to prevent the new ones from sticking.

5. Serve with all the trimmings (as below), a good grind of sea salt and black pepper, and top with whatever fresh herbs you have at hand.

ALL THE TRIMMINGS, ALL AT ONCE

If you're trying to make the perfect hash browns, it makes sense for the rest of your fry-up to be as easy as possible. Simply preheat the oven to 200°C (400°F), toss 4 sausages, 2 Spanish onions (halved) and a punnet of button mushrooms into a baking dish and splash with olive oil. Sprinkle with salt, black pepper and finely chopped mixed herbs. Cook for 10 minutes, then add 8 bacon rashers (rolled up and pinned with a cocktail stick) and 4 Roma tomatoes (halved). Bake for another 10 minutes, or until the mushrooms and tomatoes are soft.

BAD HASH BROWNS

If you've ever been served uniformly sized, uniformly coloured and uniformly tasteless hash browns at your local café, then you can bet they came straight from the freezer and into the fryer. Shop-bought hash browns might be convenient for a lazy chef, but they are packed with ingredients the home cook would never dream of adding—including antioxidants, emulsifiers, acidity regulators, preservatives and modified corn starch—and they're about as tasty to eat as a sponge.

Really, how hard is it to grate potatoes? Because that's essentially all hash browns are—grated potatoes, mixed with a few herbs, seasoned well and fried till golden brown. Accept no substitute. Unless you have some leftover perfectly mashed potato (see page 65), which works almost as well as the grated raw variety.

Mashed potato hash browns are cooked exactly the same way as described above and, as mash is great at binding together other ingredients, you can also add tasty extras, such as finely chopped spring onions or grated cheese.

BAKED BEANS

If you've only ever had baked beans out of a can, then home-cooked baked beans will be a revelation, combining meaty juices from ham or bacon bones, together with loads of seasoning and spices, and not an E-number in sight. The thick, red tomato sauce that coats the beans is also a world apart from the watery pink gravy you'll find in commercial versions.

The first food to ever be tinned, baked beans fed US soldiers during the American Civil War in the 1860s and have gone on to establish themselves as a meal-in-one mainstay for campers, poverty-stricken students and late-night pantry raiders. Mainly for their convenience—hell, you don't even have to heat them up if you're really hungry—but also for their powerful nutritional punch. Goodies found in the humble bean include protein, fibre, iron, calcium and low GI carbohydrates.

Funnily enough, baked beans aren't actually baked, but are the result of long soaking and then slow stewing on the stovetop. You can almost use any type of bean for this dish—dried pulses that is, not the fresh green ones—think haricot, navy, borlotti and cannellini. And yes, I know tinned pulses are very convenient, but this recipe really does rely on everything bubbling away together to get the depth of flavour. If you do opt for the tinned variety, you'll need to cook the ham hock by itself, and simply add the beans at the end to allow them to warm through—they are already cooked, so you don't want them to disintegrate into mush.

If speed and convenience are what you're after, think about making an industrial quantity, ladling into individual portion sizes and freezing for those mornings when you simply can't be bothered to make anything on the spot. Serve on buttered toast or with crusty bread to mop up the sauce—chunks torn from a fresh, warm baguette are perfect.

SERVES 4

Ingredients

300g dried beans

1 ham hock, fat and skin taken off and discarded

2 teaspoons olive oil

1 onion, finely chopped

2 garlic cloves, finely chopped

3 cups passata (tomato pasta sauce)

½ cup water

Method

1. Place the beans in a large bowl, cover with water and allow to soak overnight.

2. The next morning, place the beans and trimmed ham hock in a large stockpot and cover with water. Bring to the boil, reduce the heat and simmer for about 30 minutes.

3. Remove the ham hock and set aside. Scoop out 1 cup of the cooking liquid and set that aside, too. Then drain the beans.

BAKED BEANS

1 tablespoon maple syrup

½ teaspoon ground ginger

1 teaspoon smoked paprika

salt and black pepper

2 tablespoons fresh flat-leaf parsley, chopped

4. In the same pot, heat the olive oil over medium heat and cook the onion and garlic until soft. Add the passata, water, maple syrup and spices to the saucepan and stir until well combined.

5. Cut the meat from the ham hock and shred finely. Return the shredded ham and beans to the pot and simmer the whole lot together for 30 minutes until the sauce has thickened and the beans are soft. If using tinned pulses, add them at this stage and allow them to warm through. Taste them—if there is still a bit of bite left in them, they'll need a little more cooking.

6. When the beans are tender and the sauce is thick, season with salt and pepper, and stir through the parsley, leaving a little aside to sprinkle on top when you serve.

VARIATIONS ON THE THEME

Swap the ham hock for a couple of bacon bones—you'll get the flavour but not the meaty bits. Add some chilli, a splash of Worcestershire sauce or a dollop of Dijon mustard for extra bite. For a veggie version, swap the ham or bacon for carrot and celery. Golden syrup or even molasses can be used in place of the maple syrup, but only use a dessertspoonful as you don't want the flavour to be overpowering.

BAD BAKED BEANS

I can't think of a way in which you could seriously stuff up baked beans, unless, for some strange reason, you decide to add some of those nasty pink plastic frankfurters. I'd say yes to chorizo or even top-quality snags, but no to anything that is primarily made out of additives, food colouring and sawdust.

Otherwise, the only way in which baked beans could be considered bad is for their—ahem—embarrassing results. According to the unfortunate scientists who conducted a close study of this matter, when bacteria in the lower intestine break down oligosaccharides (a carbohydrate) in the baked beans, sizeable amounts of gas are produced. Rumour has it that adding cumin, caraway or coriander seeds to the beans can reduce the side effects, but perhaps that's just an ill wind…

BREAKFAST

PANCAKES

Don't just save pancakes for Shrove Tuesday (the last day of feasting before Lent), think about having them for breakfast, or as a quick snack or a fun dessert.

The first recorded recipe comes from the Roman food writer Apicius, who describes a batter of eggs, milk, water and flour that was fried and served with honey and pepper (which makes lemon and sugar sound somewhat unadventurous). Today, international variations on the theme include *báo bing* (the limp rice discs used to wrap Peking duck, often made with rice flour), pikelets, lace-thin French *crêpes*, Indian *pooris*, Galician *filloas* (sometimes made with congealed pig's blood instead of milk), drop scones, *latkes* (traditionally eaten during the Jewish Hanukkah festival), blinis and the mother of them all, Ethiopian *injeras*, which are so big and doughy they do double duty as a plate.

Thin, French-style *crêpe* pancakes can be prepared in a variety of ways—some aficionados insist on using cream instead of milk, others use beer or cider (as they do in Brittany), some say an extra egg should be added to the mix to create a richer texture. Whatever way, the batter should be smooth and free of lumps, and about the consistency of cream. Rest the batter before cooking—this results in a smoother, more uniform liquid with fewer bubbles, but don't worry if you don't have time.

Here is my favourite recipe for pancakes, resulting in thin (a few millimetres thick), lightly golden circles. For American-style fluffy hotcakes, see page 16.

MAKES 15 PANCAKES

Ingredients

125g plain flour

salt

1 free-range egg

225ml full-cream milk

small knob of butter

Method

1. Sift the flour into a large mixing bowl and add a pinch of salt. Make a hollow in the centre, and plop the egg into it. Mix the egg with a little of the flour, then add the milk.

2. Whisk the flour into the liquid ingredients, drawing it gradually into the middle until you have a smooth paste the consistency of thin cream. Cover and refrigerate for at least half an hour.

3. Heat a frying pan until it is hot enough that the batter sizzles when it hits it. (Flick a single drop of batter in to see whether the pan is ready.) If it is, wipe the frying pan with a buttered piece of kitchen towel—you only need a slick of grease across the bottom of the pan.

4. Spread a small ladleful of batter across the bottom of the pan, quickly swirling to coat. Aim for a pool of batter about 12-15cm in diameter. Any larger, and you'll have more trouble flipping it.

5. When the pancake begins to set, loosen the edges with a thin spatula and take a peek underneath. When it has just begun to colour, flip it over with the spatula and cook for another 30 seconds. If you're feeling confident, you can also toss the pancake after loosening it: firmly grasp the handle of pan with both hands, then jerk the pan up and slightly towards you—not forgetting to catch the pancake as it lands!

6. Take heart if your first pancake doesn't flip properly— it's part of pancake lore that the first one is always a disaster. Just give the pan another swipe with buttered kitchen towel and try again. You will improve as you go.

GREAT WAYS WITH PANCAKES

* Roman style with honey and black pepper.
* The old favourite—a sharp squeeze of lemon juice sweetened by a drift of white sugar. Doused in maple syrup with a side of crispy smoked bacon. The real maple syrup, mind, not the nasty flavoured product.
* Ice cream and fresh berries, poached in a little sugar until their juices begin to ooze.
* Whipped butter. Better yet, whipped butter with brandy and nutmeg.
* Rolled around smoked salmon and cream cheese, whizzed with fresh dill and finely grated lemon zest.
* With homemade jam (see page 142) and pillows of softly whipped cream

BAD PANCAKES

In my view, there's no such thing as a crap pancake. Whether tattered and torn—as the first one so often is—or scooped off the floor after an over-enthusiastic toss, they still taste great.

The only real way you can screw up a pancake is to leave lumps in the batter, or to overcook it (you don't want any charred black spots). Make sure you eat them as soon as possible, before they go rubbery. If you're cooking for a crowd, layer them between pieces of kitchen paper as you make them and keep them warm until you're ready to serve.

POACHED EGGS

To hear some people go on, you'd think poaching an egg was a dark art. And while there is a whiff of magic about creating the perfect poached egg, quite frankly, it's a doddle once you get the hang of it. Adding a squirt of lemon juice or vinegar to the water helps the white set quickly around the yolk. Do this and half the battle is won. The other secret is to use the freshest eggs you can lay your hands on as the yolks of old eggs are more likely to break up. You can check how fresh your eggs really are by breaking one gently into a saucer—the white should be thick and gooey, and the yolk bright and intact. If the egg white is watery and just kind of slumps in the saucer, puddling away from the yolk, then you know you've got an old one. Some people swear by egg poachers as a way of creating a perfect shape and keeping the white intact—the original hardworking housewife Mrs Beeton mentioned them in her iconic *Book of Household Management* as far back as 1861. Basically, these were perforated tin cups (more likely silicon these days). For my money, they're just another bit of kitchen kit that will languish at the back of your cupboard.

SERVES 2

Ingredients

½ tablespoon white vinegar or lemon juice

1 teaspoon salt

4 free-range eggs (at room temperature)

thickly sliced bread, toasted and buttered, to serve

fresh chives, chopped, to serve (optional)

salt and black pepper

Method

1. You need to cook each egg one at a time, otherwise you'll end up with a watery scramble. But first, fill a bowl with cold water and set aside. Fill a big saucepan with water to about the depth of your longest finger and add the vinegar or lemon juice and the salt.

2. Crack your eggs one at a time on to a saucer and check that they are fresh.

3. Bring the water in the saucepan to the boil then turn down a smidge until it is just simmering, with small bubbles rising from the base of saucepan.

4. Using a wooden spoon, stir the simmering water in one direction to create a whirlpool (this will help give your poached eggs a neat shape).

5. Slide your egg from the saucer into the centre of the whirling water, as close to the water as you can. Cook for 2-3 minutes for a soft yolk or 3-4 minutes for a firm yolk, but do not stir during this time.

POACHED EGGS

6. Using a slotted spoon, transfer the egg to the bowl of cold water (this stops the cooking process). Remove and drain on a plate lined with kitchen towel. Scoop out any foam from the water then repeat the process with the remaining eggs.

7. When you're ready to eat, add all the eggs to a clean pan of boiling water. Remove from the heat, cover and let them sit for 1 minute to warm through. Then take them out and drain them on kitchen towel again.

8. Serve the eggs on toast, sprinkled with chives and seasoned to taste with salt and black pepper, or try one of the suggestions below.

GREAT THINGS TO DO WITH A POACHED EGG

Poached eggs are brilliant with all kinds of extras on the side—try them with cured meats, soft cheeses, roasted tomatoes, potato-based salads, field mushrooms, avocados, pesto and more.

Serve on a bed of steamed asparagus spears, sprinkled with chunks of marinated feta or goat's curd. Toast an English muffin and top with crisp salad leaves, drizzled with a splash of your favourite dressing. Plonk a poached egg and a crispy bacon rasher on top, and there's brunch or slide onto a bed of wilted spinach, sprinkle with parmesan shavings and freshly ground black pepper.

Top with hollandaise sauce (see page 132) for eggs Florentine. For eggs Benedict, toast thick slices of baguette, butter, top with slices of ham, poached eggs and hollandaise sauce. Sprinkle with chives and serve.

BAD POACHED EGGS

You'll know your poached egg has gone wrong if it disintegrates in the water, leaving you with a lacy froth of egg white and a few clumps of yolk. Or if it bounces when you drop it into the water. But follow the directions above, keep an eye on the clock and all will be well. If your egg looks a little, well, tatty around the edges, it's not the end of the world. Take a leaf out of your local café's book and simply trim off any stray filaments, leaving you with a gleaming white circle of poached perfection.

BREAKFAST BARS

Sometimes when you roll out of bed, late again, it can be hard to motivate yourself to eat a healthy breakfast. But there's a lot to be said for making some kind of effort to fuel your body so that it's ready for the day ahead.

First of all, unless you are an inveterate midnight snacker, it's probably been hours since you last ate. Your blood sugar levels will be low and you'll be more tempted to pig out on unhealthy snacks if you skip breakfast. You might even be tempted to settle for a commercially produced breakfast bar—cereal bar, energy bar, call it what you will—that are designed to tempt the time-poor and downright lazy with the promise of convenience. But convenience comes at a cost, half of which is probably the pretty packaging.

For a fraction of the price, these homemade breakfast bars are the perfect alternative—they can be eaten with one hand as you hasten out the door and are packed full of nutritious goodness. You'll get the quick burst of energy you need from the fruits and honey, plus slow-burning energy from wholegrain cereals like the rolled oats.

Wholegrains are rich in antioxidants and minerals, and provide dietary fibre. Scientific evidence also suggests that wholegrain cereals can help protect against heart disease and some cancers. And while we are on the subject of health, I've omitted the chocolate bits that make commercial breakfast bars such a hit with kids, but if you must, then add some in place of some of the dried fruit. You can use whatever kind of seeds, nuts and fruit you like—just make sure to stick to the total quantities given below so you don't end up with a rock-solid bar that will have you dashing for the dentist.

MAKES 12 BARS

Ingredients

1 cup rolled oats

1 cup desiccated coconut

½ cup wheatgerm

1½ cups mixed seeds and nuts (sesame, sunflower and/or pumpkin seeds, pistachios, whatever you want—just make sure they are unsalted)

1 cup chopped dried fruit (sultanas, currants, dried cranberries, apricot)

Method

1. Grease and line a 3cm x 16cm x 28cm oblong baking tray with baking paper.

2. Toast the rolled oats, coconut, wheatgerm, seeds and nuts in an unoiled frying pan over medium heat, stirring constantly, for 8 to 10 minutes or until golden. Transfer to a large bowl and set aside to cool. Stir in the dried fruit.

3. Cook the butter, honey and sugar in a small saucepan over medium heat, stirring, for 3-4 minutes or until the sugar has completely dissolved. Bring to the boil. Reduce heat to low. Simmer, without stirring, for around 7 minutes or until mixture forms a soft ball when a little is dropped into ice-cold water. Add to the dry ingredients and stir until well combined.

BREAKFAST BARS

125g butter

½ cup honey or maple syrup

⅓ cup brown sugar

4. Spoon the mixture into pan and use a spatula or large metal spoon to press down the mix firmly. Allow to cool, then cut into squares or bars. These breakfast bars can be stored in an airtight container for up to 7 days, so that's breakfast sorted for the week!

ADDED CRUNCH, ADDED INGREDIENTS

* The recipe given here is for thick, soft bars—which I happen to prefer—but if you are looking for a crunchier texture, then baking is the answer. Heat the butter, honey and sugar together until just melted (don't worry about cooking for 7 minutes), then pour into the dry ingredients and mix well. Tip into a tray and bake in a preheated 170°C (325°F) oven for 25-35 minutes. Cut into bars while still hot. Once cooked and cooled, the bars can also be crumbled to make a crunchy yoghurt or ice cream topping.

* For variety, swap the honey for golden syrup or treacle—brushing warmed golden syrup over the top of the bars about 10 minutes before the end of the baking time gives the outside a sweet crust. If you decide to experiment with using fresh fruit instead of dried, you might need to play around with the quantities as the moisture content of fresh fruit is higher than dried.

BAD BREAKFAST BARS

Cereal bars, muesli bars, breakfast bars... however they are labelled, most commercial bars should more accurately be called fat, sugar and chemical bars. The only thing healthy about them is their image, with the very worst of the commercial ones containing more than 20 per cent sugar and carrying more fat than a packet of crisps or bacon and eggs fry-up. Even the fruit you see on the brightly coloured packaging can be misleading, often being a laboratory confection of chemicals and sugar rather than the real deal.

Manufacturers depend on sugar for taste and to hold the bar together—that's the sucrose, glucose or glucose syrup in the ingredients list. Then they add fat to make it even tastier. This is okay if it's just a bit of canola oil or another polyunsaturated vegetable oil, but many bars contain palm oil or coconut oil, both of which are high in artery-clogging saturated fats. Of course, some bars are better than others, but there's no denying that it's far more rewarding to make your own, not to mention a darn sight more cost effective.

MUFFINS

In the UK and Ireland, the word muffin is used to describe round, flat, yeast-leavened bread rolls, which are traditionally split and toasted, then quickly buttered and eaten hot, usually with jam. During the Victorian era, these afternoon tea staples were sold in the street by 'muffin men'—wandering traders who carried trays on their heads, ringing a handbell to advertise their approach. Once a fixture of everyday life, the humble muffin man even had a nursery rhyme written about him, and was mentioned in Jane Austen's early 19th-century novel, *Persuasion*.

But while English muffins can certainly be enjoyed at breakfast time, the version I'm talking about here are the American ones—fluffy, puffy cakes that are cooked in deep patty or muffin tins, and are leavened with baking powder rather than yeast.

American-style muffins first started taking over the world in the 1990s, and where cupcakes once held sway in the café display, muffins now rule. To get the authentic American spilling-over-the-sides muffin look, you need to fill the muffin holes more than usual—about three-quarters full should do it. Make sure you grease the entire top of the pan as well as the holes, so you can easily remove them. Placing the muffin pan on top of a baking sheet before you slide it into the oven will also help catch any overflow.

MAKES 12 LARGE MUFFINS

Ingredients

220g self-raising flour (wholemeal, if you insist)

½ cup sugar (brown, normal or castor)

1¼ cup ingredients of choice (see Flavour Variations)

1 teaspoon spices or herbs (see Flavour Variations)

¾ cup full-cream milk

1 egg

¾ cup vegetable oil

Method

1. Grease the muffin trays with a squirt of cooking oil or rub all over with a piece of buttered kitchen towel. Preheat oven to 180°C (350°F).

2. Mix all the dry ingredients together, including any flavourings such as spices or herbs.

3. In a separate bowl, whisk together the milk, egg, oil and any wet ingredients such as raspberries or mashed banana. Tip into the dry ingredients and mix roughly until you end up with a gloopy batter. Don't worry if there are still lumps—it will turn out fine, and the worst thing you can do is overmix it.

4. Divide the mix between the muffin holes and bake for 20 minutes (depending on the size of the muffin holes). You want the muffins to rise and spill over the sides of the pan.

5. Remove from the oven and leave in the pan for another 10 minutes, then turn out onto a wire rack to cool. Serve any way you want—who needs to be told how to eat a muffin?

FLAVOUR VARIATIONS

Practically anything is possible here so let your taste buds dictate your choice:

* 1 cup raspberries, fresh or frozen, with ¼ cup white chocolate buttons.
* 1¼ cups apple, diced (don't worry about peeling) with a sprinkling of cinnamon.
* 1¼ cups blueberries, fresh or frozen.
* 1 cup dried apricots, chopped, with ¼ cup shredded coconut.
* ¾ cup sultanas with ½ cup toasted walnuts, roughly chopped, and 1 teaspoon nutmeg.
* 1 cup banana, diced, with 1 tablespoon preserved ginger, chopped finely.
* Finely grated zest of 2 whole oranges with ¾ cup dark chocolate buttons.

If your appetite is for something more savoury, omit the sugar in the recipe above and replace with a pinch of salt and a good sprinkle of freshly ground black pepper. Great savoury combinations include:

* 1 cup grated cheddar or other sharp cheese, with 1 teaspoon dried mixed herbs or 1 dessertspoon fresh basil, parsley or oregano, finely chopped. Thinly sliced Roma tomatoes make a pretty topping.
* ⅓ cup finely chopped onion (spring or brown), ⅓ cup diced bacon or ham and ⅓ cup grated cheese.
* 1 cup roasted pumpkin with ⅓ cup feta, crumbled, and a sprinkling of oregano.

BAD MUFFINS

One of the joys of the muffin is that it makes a brilliant carrier for all kinds of flavourings, but whatever ingredients you decide to use, make sure not to overload the mix. As a rough guide, for 220g of flour, you should have slightly less in weight of fruit or other ingredients. That means about 1 large pear or apple for a batch of muffins. You want your little light cakes to be studded with surprises; the apple or pear shouldn't be the main event.

Muffin-making is often a case of trial and error. If your cakes come out dry, chances are you overmixed the batter, cooked them for too long or at too high a heat, or didn't quite get the flour-to-wet ingredients ratio right. Similarly, soggy, sunken muffins indicate that there was too much liquid in your batter. Experiment, and you will get there!

SNACKS

CROQUE MONSIEUR 34
CROQUETTES 36
SANDWICHES 38
PIZZA 40
QUICHE 42
CHICKEN NUGGETS 44

CHAPTER 2

SNACKS

From something you rustle up to assuage hunger pangs before dinner, to lunch on the run, finger food at a party or something for elevenses, snacks are a major part of most of our diets. Hell, some of us eat more snacks than meals.

Do not think of snacks and sandwiches as something that is a substitute for real food. If done well, they are real food.

CROQUE MONSIEUR

Only the French could take something as simple as a ham and cheese toasty and elevate it to the status of a national emblem. This very early version of fast food first appeared on a Parisian café menu on the Boulevard des Capucines in 1910 and soon gained cult status—even gaining a mention in volume two of Proust's *Remembrance of Things Past* in 1918. The name literally translates to 'crunchy mister', and why on earth it's called this is anyone's guess.

At the heart of the *croque monsieur* is nutty-tasting gruyère cheese and lean ham. These are sandwiched between slices of buttered bread—crusts removed please—that are simply lightly browned in a frying pan or under the grill. More elaborate versions are coated with a cheesy béchamel sauce (see page 130) and grilled. When served with a poached or fried egg on top, it's known as a *croque madam*.

SERVES 6-8

Ingredients

4 slices bread, crusts removed and well buttered

1 tablespoon Dijon mustard (optional)

8 thin slices gruyère cheese

8 thin slices lean ham

béchamel sauce (see page 130), with extra gruyère cheese melted in it (optional)

Method

1. Place 1 slice of bread butter-side down, spread with Dijon mustard (if using) and fill with 2 slices each of the cheese and ham. Top with the second slice of bread (butter-side up this time), then assemble the second sandwich in the same way.

2. If using the béchamel sauce, simply dollop over the top of each sandwich and grill.

3. If doing a non-saucy version, you can either cook it under the grill, or in butter in a frying pan, turning once so that both sides are golden and the cheese is melted. Serve hot.

A LOAD OF CROQUES

Versions of the sandwich with substitutions or additional ingredients are given names modelled on the original French *croque monsieur*, for example:

★ *Croque provençal* Made with the addition of slices of fresh tomato.
★ *Croque auvergnat* A cheese feast oozing with yummy Bleu d'Auvergne cheese that, for ease of shopping, can be substituted with any blue cow's milk cheese.
★ *Croque gagnet* Contains a kick due to the addition of Gouda cheese and chunks of *andouille* sausage—a spicy, smoked sausage typically used in Creole cooking. Try making it with chorizo or a German *bratwurst*.
★ *Croque Norvégien* Leave out the slices of lean ham and use smoked salmon instead.
★ *Croque tartiflette* The additions in this version turn the popular snack into a pretty substantial meal—sliced new potatoes and Reblochon (a cow's milk cheese with a yellow washed rind, made in the French Alps). But in fact any camembert or brie-style cheese can act as an appropriate substitute.
★ *Croque bolognese* Made with the addition of a delicious rich, meaty bolognese sauce.
★ Finally, the slightly less appetising Croque McDo sandwich. Sold at McDonald's locations across France, it consists of two slices of emmental cheese and a slice of ham toasted between two hamburger buns—surely the ultimate fast-food endorsement?!

BAD CROQUE MONSIEUR

Perfection comes from perfect ingredients. So while you could theoretically make a *croque monsieur* with supermarket-bought white bread and individually wrapped slices of cheese and processed ham, it's a far cry from the Paris original. Head to your local baker's and buy a French or Italian-style loaf (not a baguette and certainly not a soft spongy white loaf).

You should also make sure that the top is well grilled—a cheese toasty covered in an uncooked eiderdown of white sauce lacks a certain '*je ne sais quoi*', and certainly doesn't have any of the flavour oomph of its toasted brethren. And serve hot while you're at it. No matter how delicious the ingredients, how artful the technique, if you leave a *croque* to go cold, it's inevitably rubbery and tasteless.

CROQUETTES

Once you've mastered the perfect béchamel sauce (see page 130), this perfect little snack is a doddle to prepare.

Essentially, a croquette is a golden crumbed morsel, stuffed with a velvety sauce and your key ingredient of choice—maybe cooked fish, salted cod, ham, poultry, prawns, mushrooms or even truffles, if you've just won the lottery. In which case, you should be eating these in France or on your private jet. Then you chill the mixture until it is solid, form your shapes, crumb and fry them.

Any flavouring ingredient, such as ham, needs to be chopped very finely so that it almost becomes one with the sauce—you're after a silky filling, not lumps. If you like, you can intensify the flavour of the sauce by replacing part of the milk with a strong savoury stock, and possibly adding some very finely diced onions that have been cooked to melting point in butter.

For ideal results, you need to make the mixture a good five hours before serving—the day before would be ideal. You can even freeze the croquettes un-fried, which makes party day even easier. If the mixture is spread out in a thin layer on a flat tray, such a large glass baking dish, you will need to refrigerate it for less time.

Your choice of breadcrumbs will affect the finished croquette: Japanese panko breadcrumbs give a rougher, more textured look; standard packet breadcrumbs, a more uniform coating. It's important not to skip the step of flouring the croquette mix, as this layer of starch draws the moisture away from the food so that it doesn't turn into steam during cooking and blow the crumb off the croquette.

MAKES 14, DEPENDING ON SIZE

Ingredients

100g ham, finely diced (Spanish jamón is perfect)

1 cup mozzarella, grated

500ml thick béchamel sauce (see page 130)

Method

1. Stir the ham and cheese into the béchamel sauce and season to taste. Pour into a large shallow tray and refrigerate until cold and quite solid.

2. With floured hands, take 2 tablespoons of the mix and shape into croquettes, about 3cm wide and 6cm long.

salt and black pepper

1 cup flour

1 egg, lightly beaten

100g Japanese panko breadcrumbs

vegetable oil, for deep-frying

sea salt flakes, to sprinkle

3. Dip each croquette firstly in the flour, then the egg, then finally the crumbs.

4. Heat about 10cm of oil in a large saucepan over medium heat until a bread cube dropped into the oil turns golden in 10-15 seconds.

5. Fry, in batches depending on the size of your pan, for about 5 minutes, turning once or twice to ensure even browning. Drain on kitchen towel, transfer to a serving platter and sprinkle with sea salt flakes. Resist the temptation to bite into a croquette too quickly as you risk burning your mouth on the hot filling.

FINE FILLINGS

⋆ Chopped garlic chives and diced mushrooms.
⋆ A handful of sharp, grated cheddar cheese and a few slivers of sweet and sticky caramelised onions.
⋆ Cubed pieces of poached chicken breast or salted cod.
⋆ Slices of smoked salmon or, if you are feeling adventurous, smoked eel.
⋆ A few pre-cooked mussels, cut into manageable chunks.
⋆ Cooked rice with sweated onions.
⋆ Small chunks of feta and fresh herbs, snipped small.

You can also add extra depth to your choice of filling by providing guests with a dipping sauce cunningly chosen to complement the flavour of the croquettes.

Think a spicy tomato sauce with cheese and onions, or a lemon and garlic-infused aioli (see page 140) with smoked salmon—perfect party fare. Just make sure that the sauce is thin enough for dipping purposes—chunky relishes won't coat the croquette sufficiently.

BAD CROQUETTES

Not much can go wrong here aside from dodgy flavouring choices—I'm not sure I could stomach *croquettes à la viennoise* made with poached lambs' sweetbreads.

Overcooking croquettes to charcoal extinction is a danger, but you should also be wary of having the oil too cold. When food is fried at too low a temperature, the oil seeps into the filling before the crust has a chance to set and the end result is greasy, not crunchy.

SANDWICHES

Sandwiches may not be haute cuisine, but they're certainly easy to make, highly portable and pretty darn convenient to eat. Indeed, legend has it that it was the Earl of Sandwich, reluctant to stop playing cribbage or get grease on the cards from his sticky paws, who ordered his valet to bring him some meat between two bits of bread. Soon the phrase: "I'll have what he's having" spread like wildfire among the English aristocracy and the sandwich was born.

But a perfect sandwich is much more than two bits of bread and some filling. First up, you need to think about the bread. Crisp, crusty bread with a soft crumb is the ideal foundation for the perfect sandwich. Plain white, wholemeal, sourdough or rye, the choices are virtually endless, but a real sandwich is always made from loaf bread.

Second comes the butter (no margarine here, please). This serves two purposes—helping the filling stick to the bread, and also creating a waterproof layer so that the filling doesn't soak into the bread and make it go soggy.

Personal taste may dictate what you put inside, but sandwich architecture is just as important as the ingredients. According to researchers from America's National Institute for Agricultural Research, taste testers unanimously preferred sandwiches when strong-smelling ingredients like smoked salmon or whiffy cheese were placed at the bottom, beneath any other fillers or salads. Scientifically, the reason for this is that the upper layers prevent the smell from entering the nasal passages at the roof of the mouth, which would taint the flavour.

Contrast is the key to the filling—ideally you'll have a bit of moisture from a sauce or relish to help carry the flavours to your taste buds. You also need a bit of crunch from salad leaves or nuts so you don't feel like you're chewing on play dough.

MAKES 30-40 BITE-SIZED SANDWICHES

Ingredients

325g roasted chicken—a combination of light and dark meat, skinned and chopped finely—see page 114

120g toasted pine nuts, cooled

½ cup mayonnaise, or to taste—see page 140

CHICKEN RIBBON SANDWICHES

Method

1. Place the diced chicken and pine nuts in a mixing bowl. Mix the mayo with the tarragon, then add just enough of the mayo mix to the chicken to create a spreadable consistency.

2. Scatter the rocket leaves over half of the bread slices and pile the chicken mayonnaise over the rocket leaves. Place another slice of bread over the chicken and press down lightly.

1 tablespoon fresh tarragon, chopped (or parsley at a pinch)

100g rocket leaves (or watercress)

1 thin-sliced loaf of brown or white bread (or a mix for contrast)

cherry tomatoes, to serve

3. Trim the crusts off each sandwich, then cut into 'ribbons'.

4. Arrange neatly on a serving platter and garnish with a few spare rocket leaves and sliced cherry tomatoes. Serve immediately.

YANKEE DOODLE NOT-SO DANDY

With their BLTs, club and peanut butter and jelly sandwiches, the Americans have done their best to put their very own stamp on this snack. Take the New England Fluffernutter, as another example, a tooth-rotting confection made with two slices of bread layered with peanut butter and marshmallow fluff (out of a jar!) and possibly a banana.

Americans also gave the world the Dagwood (named after the 1930s comic-strip character), a multilayered sandwich assembled from a mountainous pile of leftovers and whatever ingredients were in the pantry at the time.

And then there's New Orleans' oyster po'boy—for those of us who are allergic to oysters, it's impossible to imagine eating a sandwich stuffed full of deep-fried oysters, mayo, pickles, shredded lettuce and tomato. Luckily, other variations are widely available, and can include prawns, fish, soft-shelled crabs, crawfish, roast beef and gravy, roast pork, meatballs, smoked sausage and more.

BAD SANDWICHES

Start with boring, bland or bad ingredients, and it's no surprise that you'll end up with a truly forgettable sandwich. For that reason alone, I'd steer clear of rubbery supermarket bread and opt for a proper loaf instead. And avoid stale bread at all costs. The same goes for cheese and ham—none of that plastic wrapped, pre-sliced muck here, thanks. Go for the sort of stuff you'd happily eat if served by itself, and don't think that hiding sub-standard ingredients between two bits of bread will fool anyone.

A great sandwich should never be served straight from the fridge. Allowing it to warm up to room temperature will release the flavours, making it a far more satisfactory mouthful.

SNACKS

PIZZA

Pizza is one of the world's best foods—tasty, easy to eat with your fingers and cheap to throw together (depending on your choice of toppings). Peasant food at its best. Making your own is one of the most satisfying things you can do and about the only way you can experience pizza the way nonna used to make it, short of visiting an authentic pizzeria. There are just three secrets to a really great pizza:

⋆ A good dough, rolled thinly so that the crust gets crispy—use Italian '00' flour, if you can get your hands on some. This is more finely ground than normal plain flour, and will give your dough a super-smooth texture. If not, use strong bread flour (one that is high in gluten), which will result in a lovely elastic dough.

⋆ A good tomato sauce—passata might be convenient, but it's no substitute for a tangy homemade sauce (see Perfect Pizza Sauce).

⋆ A limited amount of toppings—too much and you'll ruin all your hard work with the crust.

MAKES 4 MEDIUM-SIZED, THIN-CRUST PIZZAS

Ingredients

1 tablespoon dried yeast

350ml warm (not hot) water

2 tablespoons olive oil

500g '00' or strong bread flour

pinch of salt

Method

1. Add the dried yeast to the warm water, stir until it's dissolved then set aside for about 5 minutes. Add the olive oil and give it a good stir.

2. Place the flour and a pinch or 2 of salt in a mixing bowl. Add the yeast liquid and stir with a wooden spoon to combine. Then use your hands to continue mixing until a soft dough forms.

3. Remove the dough and knead it on a floured work surface. It's ready when it doesn't stick to your hands anymore and is smooth and elastic. Form into a rough ball.

4. Slosh a little olive oil into the mixing bowl. Place the dough ball in the bowl, and turn once to coat in the olive oil.

5. Cover the bowl with a tea towel and set aside in a warm place until the dough has roughly doubled in size—this can take about 2 hours, depending on the temperature.

6. Once risen, squash the dough down to remove the air bubbles and tip it out onto a floured surface. Divide into 4 parts and form each into a ball. Then use a rolling pin to roll these balls out into a pizza base (however thick you like it).

7. When ready to cook, dollop a few tablespoons of pizza sauce on the pizza base and spread evenly with the back of a spoon. Top with your choice of toppings, and bake in a preheated 200°C (400°F) oven until the base is crispy and topping golden.

PERFECT PIZZA SAUCE

Wars have probably been fought over the perfect pizza sauce, but to my mind it needs to be a garlicky, herby paste that's rich with tomatoes and almost solid enough to spread with a knife. For a quick and simple sauce, crush 2 garlic cloves into a small bowl, tip in about ¼ cup of lovely olive oil, and add several tablespoons of tomato paste. Season with lots of herbs—oregano and fresh basil are perfect—and a good sprinkling of black pepper. Fresh or dried chilli flakes can also be added if you like it hot. Mix together, adding a little more olive oil if the sauce looks too stiff.

BAD PIZZA

Bad pizza generally arrives on the back of a motorbike, thereby ensuring that even if it left the oven hot and crispy, it will be soggy and only warmish by the time you sink your teeth into it. Bad pizza is also often a far cry from the traditional peasant dish with its chewy, yet crunchy crust and its restrained layer of topping. Avoid pizzas that are overloaded with toppings. The same goes for those soft, thick, doughy bases that seem like a good idea at the time, but will leave you clutching your belly for hours afterwards. And bad pizzas seem to be proliferating—whoever came up with the idea for the stuffed crust pizza should be shot. Also the person who thought that pizzas deserved the fusion food treatment—chicken tikka is NOT a pizza topping!

If making your own, don't overload it—flavours get lost and too much topping can make it difficult to get the base to cook. You also need to have a really hot oven to get the base crispy. The cooking time depends on the thickness of the base and the amount of topping, so check your pizza regularly and rotate if necessary to cook it evenly.

QUICHE

Larousse Gastronomique, the bible of all things French and foody, describes quiche Lorraine as: "an open tart filled with a mixture of beaten eggs, fresh cream and pieces of bacon, served hot as a first course or *hors d'oeuvre*." It gets its name from the region it came from (Lorraine, duh), but locally it's known as *féouse*.

To keep the base crisp, it's a good idea to brush the pastry with a little egg white, before adding the filling. Blind baking (explained in the method) the base will help you avoid the most common of issues—overcooked filling and undercooked pastry. By doing this, you get the pastry well under way before the filling goes in.

You should also plan on using a deep tin rather than a shallow flan tin, if possible. This will help you achieve the lovely just-set wobble you're after—aim for about 3cm of filling.

Whisking the filling is critical—this suspends the ingredients in the custard; alternatively, you can try dropping in about half of them just before you slide the quiche into the oven. That way, some will still be hanging about in the middle of the custard as it sets, rather than sinking.

SERVES 6

Ingredients

225g plain flour

pinch of salt

225g very cold butter, diced

100ml very cold or iced water

200g streaky bacon, chopped—dry-cured, smoked bacon is best

320ml double cream

4 eggs and 2 egg yolks (plus 1 egg white for brushing the pastry)

Method

1. Sift the flour and a big pinch of salt into a large bowl. Stir in the diced butter, then rub it all together so that it's crumbly.

2. Pour about half of the water into the flour/butter mix, and combine with a knife. Then add just enough extra water to bring the mixture into a ball of dough. Cover with clingfilm and leave to rest in the fridge for 20 minutes.

3. On a lightly floured work surface, shape the dough into a rectangle, then roll it out until 3 times its original length.

4. Grab the top edge of the dough and fold the top third towards the centre, then bring the bottom third up to meet it, so that your dough has 3 layers. Give the dough a quarter turn and roll out again until 3 times the length, fold again as before, and chill for a further 20 minutes.

5. Preheat the oven to 180°C (350°F). Lightly oil a 3cm-deep 20cm-diameter tin, and line it with the pastry, leaving an extra few centimetres overhang to prevent shrinkage. Line the pastry shell with foil—making sure to put the shiny side down so it doesn't stick—and weigh it down with baking beans or rice.

6. Blind bake the shell in the oven for 40 minutes, then remove the foil and beans, and patch up any holes with any leftover raw pastry (if needed). Brush the base with egg white and return to the oven for 5 minutes. Carefully trim the overhanging pastry to neaten it up.

7. Gently fry the bacon for 8–10 minutes, until it's cooked, but not crisp. Drain on kitchen towel and spread half over the hot base.

8. Put the cream, eggs and extra yolks into a large bowl with a generous pinch of salt, and beat together until frothy. Pour into the pastry shell, then sprinkle over the rest of the bacon and slide it into the oven.

9. The quiche will take about 20 minutes to cook, but keep an eye on it—it's done when it's puffed up and golden, but ever so slightly still wobbly at the centre.

GOOD VARIATIONS

Mushroom (my preference is Swiss brown), feta and spinach, prawn and garlic, smoked salmon and dill, or Mediterranean-style—roasted capsicum, zucchini, onions, artichoke hearts, black olives and sun-dried tomatoes. If you can't be bothered making the puff pastry, try shortcrust pastry (see page 148), but omit the sugar and add a pinch of salt.

BAD QUICHE

Mass production lines have done this classic French dish a grave disservice. Watery filling can be another problem. If not sticking pedantically to the classic quiche Lorraine, you can add pretty much anything you like to the custard base—cheese and leek, spinach, flaked salmon, even prawns… but you need to make sure that whatever it is won't ooze water into the pastry. This means you need to sauté ingredients such as leeks, onions and bacon, and blanche and then squeeze the liquid out of vegetables such as spinach.

If you find that the quiche looks fine, but that the whole thing deflates like a balloon on leaving the oven, it means you've cooked it too hot and too fast.

SNACKS

CHICKEN NUGGETS

Golden and crispy on the outside, and juicy on the inside, homemade chicken nuggets are simple to whip up, and can be eaten either as a snack with a spicy or tangy dip, or partnered with sides such as oven-roasted vegetables, salad, a baked potato, or a wholegrain roll for a complete meal. Best of all, these nuggets are made from good old wholesome chicken breasts, rather than 'mechanically separated chicken' as it's known in the industry. You can practically claim them as a health food.

SERVES 4

Ingredients

150g breadcrumbs (dried, not fresh)

sprinkle of seasoning (parmesan, mixed dried herbs, garlic, onion salt, for example)

2 chicken breasts, roughly chopped

salt and black pepper

1 tablespoon fresh herbs (basil or parsley, or both)

50g plain flour

2 free-range eggs, lightly whisked

100ml vegetable oil

Method

1. First, make the crumb mix by combining the breadcrumbs with your choice of seasoning in a medium-sized bowl.

2. Whiz the chicken chunks in a food processor until smooth. Season with salt and pepper, and add the fresh herbs. Pulse again until smooth.

3. On the bench, line up the chicken mix, the flour, the eggs and the breadcrumbs in 4 bowls. To shape the nuggets, rub your hands with some flour to avoid them becoming too sticky. Then take some chicken mixture and roll it in the palm of your hands to create a smooth ball shape about the size of a table tennis ball.

4. Now, take a nugget and roll it in the flour. When totally covered, roll it in the egg. Next, roll the nugget in the breadcrumbs until evenly coated. Place the nugget on a plate and gently press down on it with the flat side of a knife to form the perfect nugget shape.

5. In a large frying pan, heat the oil until it is hot but not smoking. Place the nuggets into the pan and cook gently on low heat for about 5 minutes, turning them every few minutes so they don't burn. Once cooked through, golden and crisp, drain the nuggets on kitchen towel to remove the excess oil, then serve hot with a lovely fresh salad, simply dressed veggies or a spicy dipping sauce.

GREAT VARIATIONS

Rather than mincing the chicken breast, you can also cut it into nugget shapes and coat as before. This way, not only will you preserve the texture of the breast, you will cut down on preparation time as well.

It you are looking for an even healthier option, bake the nuggets rather than frying them—they'll take about 15 minutes in a hot oven, but you need to remember to turn them over about halfway through.

You can also ring the changes by swapping the egg dip for another thickish liquid, such as mustard, barbecue sauce, tomato sauce or even mayonnaise (very handy if you've run out of eggs). Or instead of coating them in ordinary breadcrumbs, try using the larger Japanese panko crumbs, or even crushed crackers if you are all out of dried bread and really desperate for your fix of nuggets.

The crumb mix can also be flavoured with extra ingredients such as finely chopped herbs, grated parmesan cheese, or even diced red chilli and fresh coriander for a spicy, fragrant Thai take on an old family favourite.

BAD CHICKEN NUGGETS

On the devil's side of the equation lie the chicken nuggets so beloved of fast food junkies and kids. These are made, not with lovely white breast meat, but from something known as pink slime—the result of stripping chickens down to the bone, then grinding them up into a mash with stabilisers, preservatives, sugars, fats and all sorts of other nasties. This mix is then pressed into shape, breaded, deep-fried, freeze-dried, and then shipped to a fast food restaurant near you. Ewww.

SOUP

GAZPACHO 48
TOMATO SOUP 50
MINESTRONE 52
PUMPKIN SOUP 54
FRENCH ONION SOUP 56

CHAPTER 3

SOUP

Thick and chunky, thin and silky, hot or cold—there's a type of soup for every palate, country, culture and budget. As well as being an instant hit for anyone entering your house on a blustery winter's day, soups have the added advantage of often freezing quite well, so you can have delicious homemade meals ready at the drop of a hat.

One day spent at home, wandering over to the stove every now and then to give your soup a lazy stir, can equal weeks of drawn-out gustatory pleasure.

GAZPACHO

This traditional cold Spanish soup is a refreshing pick-me-up in a bowl, full of puréed raw veggies at the height of their powers and stuffed full of wonderfully fresh flavours and vitamins. In its original form, derived from the Arabs who once occupied Spain, its key ingredients were bread, garlic, olive oil, vinegar, salt and water.

In later years, tomatoes and capsicums—brought from the New World—joined the party, but garlic should still be the dominant flavour. Meanwhile, the addition of bread gives the gazpacho a creamy texture that transforms it from mere vegetable juice to something altogether more soupy.

The real secret to gazpacho, however, assuming your ingredients are obscenely ripe and your fridge is working well, is lashings of very good extra-virgin olive oil. Ideally you should use sherry vinegar—after all, gazpacho is an Andalusian dish—but red wine vinegar is acceptable, too.

As the soup is generally served ice-cold, getting the balance of flavours is important so taste it as you go, and beware of adding too much salt. Don't be tempted to chill the soup by adding ice cubes, as they'll just melt and dilute the flavours.

Choose any garnishes with care—mint and parsley leaves are good, as are diced black olives, or a finely chopped hard-boiled egg, also try small cubes of cucumber, capsicums and spring onion, or meaty Spanish ham (*jamón*).

SERVES 4

Ingredients

1kg very ripe tomatoes, diced

1 red capsicum and 1 green capsicum, deseeded and diced

1 medium cucumber, peeled and diced

2 garlic cloves, peeled and crushed

150ml extra-virgin olive oil (only the very best)

100g day-old sourdough or wood-fired bread, soaked in cold water for 15 minutes

salt and black pepper, to taste

2 tablespoons sherry vinegar (red wine vinegar will do if that's all you have)

fresh mint leaves, to garnish

Method

1. Tip the diced tomatoes, capsicums and cucumber, crushed garlic and olive oil into a food processor or blender.

2. Squeeze out the water from the bread, tear it into chunks, and add to the mixture.

3. Blend until smooth, then add the salt, pepper and vinegar to taste and whiz again.

4. Pass the mixture through a fine sieve and into a large jug, then cover and refrigerate until well chilled. Serve very cold, with mint leaves as a garnish.

GOOD FOR YOU, TOO

During the cooking process, up to 70 per cent of the water-soluble Vitamins B and C can be lost. In this classic soup, the vegetables are left raw and simply puréed, which means they retain maximum levels of vitamins and minerals.

Just make sure you don't follow the example given in Pedro Almodóvar's classic film *Women on the Verge of a Nervous Breakdown* (1986), where one of the characters adds the better part of a bottle of sleeping pills to the soup and, quite possibly, a little piece of her finger given the violence of her chopping. Yes, it may be protein, but not the sort you want to serve.

BAD GAZPACHO

Gazpacho is designed to use up summer's glut of tomatoes, cucumbers and capsicums, so it would be a travesty to make it with anaemic midwinter tomatoes or capsicums. The veggies are the stars of the show, so seek out the best possible specimens to make this worth your while.

Definitely ignore any of the 'labour-saving' recipes you might encounter that require tinned tomatoes or tomato soup as the base. Steer clear too of 'innovative' and unusual garnishes—mango pickle, prawns, chilli and cumin seeds turn up in some modern versions, but to my mind they simply spoil the punchy, garlic flavour of the original and the simple seasonal goodness of the dish.

TOMATO SOUP

A good tomato soup can be considered the little black dress of soups. Unadorned and paired with hot buttered toast, it's the ultimate comfort food. But when you dress it up with a few flash garnishes, it makes a perfect start to a swish dinner party.

For the tastiest tomato soup you'll ever experience, wait until you can get your hands on lots of tomatoes at their ripest peak. Use whatever variety you like, or a mix, ideally picked warm from your own garden, of course. A pinch of sugar added at the same time as the seasoning will help bring out their flavour, and give them an added boost if they're not quite at their best.

Although it's a bit of a fiddle, it is definitely worth peeling your tomatoes, otherwise you'll end up with stringy bits of skin in an otherwise silky soup. The simplest way to do this is to cut a cross in the bottom of each tomato and plunge into boiling water for about 30 seconds.

Remove with a slotted spoon and then plunge into a bath of ice-cold water. Then, starting at the cross in the bottom, you can then easily pull away the skin from the flesh.

SERVES 4

Ingredients

750g tomatoes, skinned and cut into quarters or eighths, depending on size

4 teaspoons salt

⅓ cup olive oil, plus 2 tablespoons to drizzle

4 onions

4 garlic cloves, peeled

1 bunch fresh basil leaves

600ml chicken stock

salt and black pepper

Method

1. Chop the tomatoes in half, sprinkle with salt and cover with the olive oil. Mix together with your hands.

2. In a large, heavy-based saucepan, cook the onions and garlic gently in the extra oil until the onion is translucent and golden; this should take about 6 minutes. Then add the tomato and oil mix, and slowly bring the lot to the boil.

3. Simmer for about 5 minutes, then add the basil leaves, stock and season to taste. Cook for another 5-10 minutes or until the tomatoes have nearly given up the ghost.

4. Remove from the heat and put the mix through a mouli or blender. Test the seasoning.

5. To serve, bring the soup to the boil, whisking boldly, then ladle into bowls and drizzle with a splash of fruity olive oil.

TOUCHES OF GENIUS

To give your tomato soup extra pop, you can roast your tomatoes first with a touch of olive oil, some garlic, fresh thyme or oregano, sea salt and black pepper. This helps concentrate the flavours wonderfully, before you then transform them into a super soup.

You can also omit the stock in the recipe here altogether, in which case you'll end up with a much more robust soup that sings only of tomatoes, or replace the stock with a mix of dry white wine and water.

Perfect accompaniments include toasted baguette, topped with butter mixed with chopped basil leaves, or perhaps some garlic-rubbed croutons made from day-old sourdough bread.

BAD TOMATO SOUP

The whole idea behind tomato soup is to concentrate fresh tomatoes down to their perfectly delicious essence. Immature, tasteless specimens from the supermarket simply won't do if you want to create a sensational soup. Go for the reddest, ripest, zingiest tomatoes you can lay your hands on.

And never, but never, think of adding cream. That'll turn a perfectly respectable tomato soup into the kind of stuff that comes out of a can.

MINESTRONE

The joy of minestrone is that is really just an excuse get as many seasonal vegetables into the one pot as possible, moistened by a flavoursome stock and bulked out with rice, beans, potatoes or pasta.

Practically everyone makes it differently, depending on what's to hand and their personal preferences. Even the bible of Italian cooking, *The Silver Spoon*, gives no fewer than 10 regional versions—including a recipe that features capsicums and eggplants from Naples; one with turnip tops and *cime di rapa* (a leafy vegetable with green buds that resemble small heads of broccoli) that is native to Puglia; and the bacon, parmesan and sage version that is so beloved by the people of Milan.

Oddly enough, for a country so obsessed with the tomato, in Italy it's not considered essential for minestrone. However, if you do decide to add a few toms, please make sure to peel them, so you don't end up with nasty red stringy bits that will catch in people's teeth. The simplest way to do this is to cut a cross in the bottom of each tomato and plunge into boiling water for about 30 seconds.

Remove with a slotted spoon and then plunge into a bath of ice-cold water. Then, starting at the cross in the bottom, you can easily pull away the skin from the flesh.

At the heart of the soup though is the stock—ideally a homemade, vegetable stock, although some prefer chicken for an added depth of flavour. You can also chuck in that rind of parmesan cheese lurking in the back of your fridge, if you like.

Starch is the other essential ingredient—from rice, pasta, beans, potatoes or a combination. You need enough to make it satisfying, but not so stodgy that the spoon can stand upright all by itself.

As for the veggies, add these in stages so they all cook to *al dente*—soft but still with a little bite. You don't want the whole thing to cook down to a vegetable sludge.

SERVES 12

Ingredients

3 tablespoons olive oil

1 onion, chopped

2 garlic cloves, crushed

2 carrots, diced (1cm cubes)

2 sticks of celery, diced

Method

1. Heat the oil in a heavy-based saucepan and add the onion and garlic. Cook gently over medium heat for 5 minutes, without allowing them to brown, then add the carrots and celery, and cook until all is soft.

2. Add the rest of your chosen vegetables in order of their cooking time (green beans will take longer than peas or zucchini, for example) and allow them to soften up a bit. Finally, stir in the potato and tomatoes.

MINESTRONE

seasonal vegetables of your choice (for this quantity: 1 zucchini, diced; a handful of fresh peas or broad beans; cabbage leaves, shredded; 3 large leaves of cavolo nero or silver beet, shredded; a handful of fresh green beans, topped and sliced diagonally into 3cm lengths)

1 potato, cut into 2cm dice

3 tomatoes, peeled and chopped

1.5 litres best-quality vegetable stock

100g cooked and drained borlotti (or cannellini) beans

salt and black pepper

100g cooked pasta (macaroni or small or broken pasta bits), drained

grated parmesan, olive oil, a few fresh basil leaves, to serve

3. Add the stock and cooked borlotti beans. Season to taste, bring to the boil, then turn down the heat and simmer for about 15 minutes until the potato is cooked. Add the cooked pasta and simmer for another few minutes until warmed through. Check the seasoning and serve hot with your choice of garnishes and some crusty rolls.

SOFFRITTO SECRETS

Soffritto (also known as *mirepoix* in France, *refogado* in Portugal and *sofregit* in Spain) is the base for so many dishes that it's definitely worth knowing about. Essentially, it's a mix of finely diced celery, carrots and onions, gently sautéed or braised in butter or oil for 15-30 minutes to soften and release the aromatic flavours.

Soffritto may also include other ingredients, such as garlic, tomato, parsley, paprika, capsicum, and so on.

BAD MINESTRONE

Try telling any Italian that you can make minestrone from chicken pot noodles, frozen diced veggies and a can of mixed beans, and you're likely to have a stiletto between your ribs before you can blink. The same is true of the powdered and tinned versions—brick red, watery but weirdly acidic and infested with tiny, white maggots of pasta. But some people will do anything to get dinner on the table in five minutes flat, and so such disasters are created. In this as in most things, convenience is the enemy of flavour—sure it's food, but not food worth eating.

PUMPKIN SOUP

Perfect pumpkin soup tastes like autumn—smoky, warm and with just a hint of the last days of summer. To intensify the flavour of your pumpkin, it's a good idea to drizzle with a little olive oil and roast in the oven until soft and slightly charred around the edges.

This adds a delicious smoky edge to the finished soup that cannot be replicated through simply boiling the pumpkin in stock. Fresh nutmeg is the other key ingredient—much more flavoursome than the dried variety, although admittedly less convenient.

SERVES 4

Ingredients

2 tablespoons olive oil

1 onion, finely chopped

1 leek, white part only, finely sliced

1 garlic clove, crushed

½ teaspoon freshly grated nutmeg

1kg pumpkin (butternut), peeled and diced—you can also roast it, as above

1 large potato, peeled and diced

1 litre best-quality chicken or vegetable stock

½ cup single cream

Method

1. Heat the oil in a large heavy-based saucepan over low heat, add the onion and leek, and cook for several minutes, until soft but not coloured. Add the garlic and nutmeg, and cook for 30 seconds, stirring all the time.

2. Toss in the pumpkin chunks, potato and stock and bring to the boil. Turn the heat down to low, cover and let simmer away for 30 minutes. Allow the mix to cool slightly, then blend in batches so that it's completely smooth and velvety.

3. Return the soup to the saucepan, stir through the cream and reheat gently. Season and add a little more nutmeg if desired.

PETER, PETER, PUMPKIN EATER

The size, shape and colour of the humble pumpkin meant it was regarded with curiosity and a sense of trepidation when first brought back to Europe from the Americas in the 1500s.

However, the strange-looking ingredient soon found its place, not so much as a food fit for humans, but as an important prop in fairy tales such as Cinderella, nursery rhymes—including the strangely entitled *Peter, Peter, Pumpkin Eater*—and pigpens across the continent.

Even today in the UK, the pumpkin is considered somewhat of an oddity as an ingredient. However, in the US and Australasia, pumpkins have long been relished as fare fit for feasting on, working equally well in savoury and sweet dishes. The sweetness of the pumpkin is easily explained once you realise that it is really a fruit, or even more accurately, a berry, albeit the only one with such a hard, outer shell.

Of course, lots of people have tried to improve upon this classic—mainly through the addition of different spices and flavourings. As delicious as some of these combinations might be, in my book, they don't equal a proper pumpkin soup. Still, should you feel like experimenting one rainy Saturday afternoon, here are some of the most common additions and variations:

- Other liquids—instead of chicken or vegetable stock, try coconut milk, dry white wine, cream, yoghurt, buttermilk, sour cream or milk.
- Other flavourings—instead of nutmeg, try chives, rosemary, tarragon, cumin, coriander, bacon, ham, cinnamon, ginger, tahini, tomato paste, lemongrass, chilli, curry powder, Thai curry paste, parsley or sage.
- Other vegetables/fruits—corn, cauliflower, tomato, apple, sweet potato.
- Other textures—bring a chunky feel to this otherwise smooth soup with lentils, beans, rice, pasta, quinoa or walnuts.

BAD PUMPKIN SOUP

Around Halloween, huge golden carving pumpkins are to be found piled-high at the supermarket and greengrocer, ready to be disembowelled and turned into grisly lanterns. Tempting as it might be to use the discarded flesh for a soup or perhaps a pumpkin pie —don't do it. Speaking from bitter experience, I found that when I whizzed up a batch of soup to feed 18, the flesh of these pumpkins is only fit for farm feed. Butternut pumpkins, on the other hand, make perfect soup.

SOUPS

FRENCH ONION SOUP

Onion soup was first recorded in recipe form back when Italians were striding around in togas. Traditionally, it was peasant food, thanks to onions being easy and cheap to grow and store, but it's also just at home in the classiest of French restaurants, given extra kudos with a splash of cognac, sherry or brandy.

Any type of onion may be used, as long as they are juicy and firm, not withered or even—god forbid—starting to sprout. Red onions are the sweetest of all. You can mix up your varieties too—no need to stick with the one type, but be aware that little ones will be very time consuming to peel. You should also use the best stock you can either make or get your hands on, and remember to taste before you add any seasonings, as stock can vary in saltiness. Beef is traditional, but chicken or vegetable also work.

The rich flavour comes from caramelising the sliced onions very slowly until the melting sugars lightly colour the onion. It's important not to let the onions brown too much, or they'll give the soup a bitter taste. Covering the pan with a lid can help, as drips from steam condensing on the inside will keep the onions moist.

When the onions are meltingly soft and just coloured—this will take at least half an hour—wine is added to deglaze the pan and add another layer of flavour and colour to the soup. It's important to skim the scum off the surface as the soup cooks, so as to remove the impurities.

SERVES 4-6

Ingredients

700g onions

40g butter

1 tablespoon olive oil

2 sprigs fresh thyme

5 garlic cloves, finely chopped

2 tablespoons flour

1.75 litres beef stock, heated to boiling point

125ml white wine

salt and black pepper

Method

1. Peel and thinly slice the onions—either by hand or in a food processor.

2. Warm the butter and a small glug of olive oil over low to medium heat, then toss in the onions, thyme and garlic, and allow the lot to cook, moving the mix around lazily with a wooden spoon every now and then. They'll be ready when they are soft enough to crush between your fingers, and when they're sticky, sweet and gold in colour.

3. Stir in a couple of tablespoons of flour and allow to cook for several minutes. Then pour in the boiling stock and white wine. Partially cover with a lid and leave to simmer for a good 45 minutes.

4. Taste for seasoning, add extra salt and pepper if needed, then ladle into deep bowls to serve.

CLASSIC CHEESE CROUTONS

Classic French onion soup is as much about presentation as flavour, so is traditionally served with cheese croutons floating on top—crispy golden slices of baguette (what else!) topped with gooey cheese. To make enough for 4 servings, take 16 thin slices of baguette, place on an oiled baking tray and drizzle with olive oil. Bake the slices in a 200°C (400°F) oven for around 4 minutes, or until they are crisp and lightly tanned.

Turn over and cook the other side to the same point, then top with around 100g grated gruyère, emmental or cheddar cheese. Return to the oven or slide under the grill and bake until melted. Use these to top the bowls of steaming soup.

BAD FRENCH ONION SOUP

The 1970s have a lot to answer for—French onion dip being possibly the worst offering invented during this experimental decade. For this, cream cheese was blended with packet onion soup to create a vile brown paste flecked with nuggets of desiccated onion.

Possibly the only thing worse is packet onion soup à la natural—reconstituted with boiling water to create a liquid resembling the dregs found in the sink after a dinner party, and tasting much the same.

The do-it-yourself version is far, far superior and pretty darn foolproof, as long as you caramelise the onions properly and don't allow them to burn. And then a quick word on ingredients—using soft or sprouted onions will lead to a bitter taste, while nasty, cheap or over-salted stock can also affect the flavour of the finished dish.

VEGETABLES

ASPARAGUS 60
EGGPLANT 62
ROAST AND MASHED POTATOES 64
CHIPS 66
AVOCADO 68
ZUCCHINI 70
VEGETABLE SALAD 72

CHAPTER 4
VEGETABLES

Vegetables, salad leaves and herbs are an often-loathed food group—particularly among toddlers and those who grew up in the days of unwieldy iceberg lettuce and cold-store tomatoes, when boiling veggies for hours was the norm, rather than stir-frying or steaming them.

When grown well and treated with respect in the kitchen, greens (and reds and oranges and purples and yellows) have a lot to offer the good cook and the hungry diner, vitamins and minerals included. Master the art of preparing a few core salads and vegetable dishes, and you're on your way to a far healthier and tastier future.

ASPARAGUS

There is a lot of twaddle talked about how to cook asparagus. Some say that you need to tie the spears together with string; others that spears must stand upright in boiling water—so that the ends are boiled, while the tips are just gently steamed. You can even waste money on a special asparagus steamer. My advice? Don't over think it!

For perfect asparagus, all you really need to do is either boil the spears in plenty of water for 3-5 minutes (depending on size), or steam them for 4-5 minutes. The end result should be bright green, crisp yet tender vegetables. Give one spear a poke with a knife to check.

If planning to toss a few spears through a fresh, seasonal salad, you should plunge the asparagus immediately into cold water to stop any further cooking and maintain the colour.

Asparagus partners beautifully with hollandaise sauce (see page 132) or hot, melted butter, or as asparagus mimosa—a traditional French bistro dish of blanched asparagus, drizzled with oil and sprinkled with capers, salt and pepper, and topped with finely grated hard-boiled eggs. It is called a mimosa because the finished dish resembles the pretty yellow-and-white flower.

You can also toss spears in olive oil and roast in a hot oven for 8-10 minutes, or grill them, as in the following recipe, which adds a deliciously nutty flavour.

GRILLED ASPARAGUS AND ZUCCHINI SALAD WITH PERSIAN FETA

SERVES 4-6

Ingredients

350g cherry tomatoes, halved

150ml olive oil mixed with 2 cloves of garlic, crushed

salt and black pepper

12 spears green asparagus

2 zucchini, thinly sliced lengthways (a mandolin makes this job a breeze)

couple of handfuls of baby rocket leaves

100g Persian feta (marinated in garlic, herbs and oil), oil reserved

fresh basil leaves, to garnish

Method

1. Preheat the oven to 170°C (325°F).

2. Mix the tomatoes with 3 tablespoons of the garlic oil and season. Toss onto a baking tray lined with baking paper and roast for 30 minutes or so, until semi-dried and exploding with flavour. Remove and allow to cool.

3. Snap off the woody ends of the asparagus and blanch for 4 minutes in a large pot of boiling water. Drain and plunge into cold water. Drain again, toss into a large mixing bowl with the sliced zucchini, the remaining olive oil and some more salt and pepper.

4. On a barbecue or very hot griddle pan, grill the zucchinis and asparagus, turning them over after 1 minute once they've developed lovely char marks.
5. To assemble, arrange the rocket, zucchini, asparagus and tomatoes on a serving platter. Scatter with basil leaves and dollops of the Persian feta, and drizzle over a little of the reserved oil from the feta.

THE SCIENCE OF STINK

Asparagus has one downside: it contains a compound called asparagusic acid, which the human body metabolises into another chemical that turns out to be, wait for it… closely related to the notoriously foul-smelling spray of the skunk. That's why, after feasting on asparagus, you may well notice a strong odour to your urine.

However, it is a bit of a genetic lottery—some people don't produce this compound at all, and others are unable to smell it.

But a bad smell is a small price to pay for a hit of healthy good stuff because, on the plus side, asparagus is high in Vitamins B6 and C, potassium, iron and calcium, plus fibre, folate and antioxidants.

BAD ASPARAGUS

There's no point throwing any old asparagus spears on the grill and hoping for the best. Asparagus is best eaten young and freshly picked, when it's at its juiciest and sweetest. The clock starts ticking the moment the spears are plucked from the ground and the longer they are stored, the tougher and less tasty this vegetable becomes.

One major word of warning—even freshly picked asparagus is likely to have a woody end that no amount of cooking or chewing can remedy. To ensure you don't end up eating these, simply bend the bottom of the stalk—there should be a natural break point, where the tough end meets the more tender portion—snap off the bottom section and discard.

EGGPLANT

When it comes to eggplant, many cooks look nervously for the nearest exit. Partly because it can be bitter and partly because if it's not cooked properly, it can be horribly bland. The bitter taste comes from the seeds, which contain nicotinoid alkaloids (yep, the eggplant is closely related to tobacco). Elderly specimens are much more likely to taste bitter, so pick glossy, firm, young eggplants.

Cut into the flesh and check what its innards look like, too—it should be pale, with not too many seeds. Dark splotchy flesh and lots of seeds are a good indicator that you'll end up with a lousy texture and taste. You can help improve this by salting your eggplant to draw off the bitter juices (see right). There are almost as many ways of cooking eggplant as there are varieties and colours—try roasting, frying, grilling, sautéing, boiling or braising, as in this delicate Thai curry, below.

THAI EGGPLANT CURRY

SERVES 4

Ingredients

3 large red chillis, deseeded and stalks removed, chopped

6 garlic cloves, chopped

3cm fresh ginger, peeled

2 lemongrass stalks, chopped

2 tablespoons ground turmeric

1 teaspoon chilli powder

1 tablespoon olive oil

2-3 eggplants (600g), quartered lengthways, then halved

1 tablespoon sugar

2 onions, finely chopped

1 tablespoon Thai fish sauce

400ml can coconut milk

300ml vegetable stock (or water)

juice of 1-2 limes

fresh coriander, to serve

Method

1. Whizz the chillis, garlic, ginger and lemongrass to a coarse paste in a food processor, and set aside. Mix the turmeric and chilli powder together and rub it all over the eggplant chunks.

2. Heat the oil in a frying pan, then brown the eggplants on all sides. Remove from the pan and set aside. Cook the paste, sugar and onions for several minutes until fragrant, then return the eggplants to the frying pan.

3. Add the fish sauce, coconut milk and stock, mix well, and bring to the boil.

4. Reduce the heat and cook gently until the eggplant is tender, but not mushy (about 15 minutes).

5. Season to taste with lime juice and more salt, if needed. Serve hot over steamed rice, topped with a generous sprinkling of chopped coriander.

PARMIGIANA DI MELANZANE

The southern Italians have their own way of using eggplants and, not surprisingly, it involves tomatoes. This popular dish is claimed by both Campania and the island province of Sicily, and contrary to popular opinion did not originate in the northern city of Parma, as the name '*parmigiana*' might suggest.

Simply fill a casserole dish with alternate layers of grilled or shallow-fried eggplant slices, a rich garlic and tomato pasta sauce (see page 77), and finely grated parmesan.

Top with breadcrumbs that have been tossed in olive oil and a teaspoon of dried herbs (try oregano or majoram), and finish with a final sprinkle of parmesan. The deliciously simple dish takes about 30 minutes in a 190°C (375°F) oven to become golden and bubbly, and is perfect by itself or served with grilled or roasted meats.

BAD EGGPLANT

The two biggest complaints about eggplant are that it can taste bitter and that it can absorb too much oil. To overcome the bitterness, you need to salt and purge the flesh. This has the added effect of helping squish the flesh so that it won't soak up too much oil.

Cut the eggplant into chunks or slices, sprinkle liberally with salt and leave in a colander for 30 minutes or so. The salt will draw out the bitter juices, and popping something heavy on top will speed up the process. Then all you have to do is rinse the chunks well, and press them dry in a clean tea towel. The harder you squish the chunks, the less oil they'll soak up during the cooking process.

Soggy fried eggplant is caused by overloading the pan so that the temperature of the oil drops and the eggplant stews rather than fries. You can also add a little water to the pan when frying eggplant so that it soaks up less oil.

A final word of warning: whether you're roasting, grilling or frying your eggplant, make sure that the flesh is almost melting, but not quite mushy. Undercooked, it can be leathery and squeaky, tasteless and unpleasant.

ROAST AND MASHED POTATOES

Little compares with the perfection of a great roast spud, with its crisp golden exterior and fluffy inside. They look simple—heck, they are simple—but there are still a few tricks to these lovely carb-laden beauties.

First, make sure you're using the right kind of spud. You need a variety that's floury rather than waxy in texture once cooked. For example: Desiree; Dutch Creams; Sebago; Royal Blue; Kipfler; Golden Wonder. Second, a spoonful of white wine vinegar or lemon juice in the parboiling water helps keep the spuds together, even if you accidentally overcook them. Third, preheat your oil. Tossing parboiled spuds in cold oil makes them go soggy.

Equally tasty and just as easy to make are mashed potatoes—see the recipe on the opposite page for more potato perfection.

SERVES 8-10

Ingredients

2kg potatoes, peeled and cut into large chunks

sea salt

1 tablespoon white wine vinegar or lemon juice

¼ cup fat or oil (goose or duck fat is the bee's knees, but you can also use chicken or bacon fat, or olive oil), hot

black pepper

handful fresh thyme sprigs

Method

1. Preheat oven to 260°C (500°F). Place the potato chunks into a large pot and just cover with water. Season with the salt and vinegar, and bring to the boil. Once boiling, lower the heat and simmer for 5-8 minutes. The outside of the spud should just give to a knife or skewer. Drain thoroughly.

2. Return the spuds to the saucepan, slosh in the hot oil or fat and shake them around until the edges are bashed up—just a little; you don't want the spuds to disintegrate completely.

3. Divide the potatoes between 2 baking trays, sprinkle with pepper and thyme. Roast for 20 minutes or until the bums of the spuds are crisp and golden. Use a spatula to turn them carefully, then return to the oven and roast for another 15 minutes, or until golden brown all over. Serve with a good sprinkle of sea salt.

Note—If you want to cook your spuds with the roast, take a scoop of fat from around the meat, add to the drained spuds and shake them in the saucepan before adding to the roasting tray, about an hour before your roast is ready to be removed from the oven. Spuds take slightly longer this way, as the oven temperature is likely to be lower to suit the meat.

ROAST AND MASHED POTATOES

SERVES 8

Ingredients

1.8kg potatoes (or sweet potatoes, or a mix of spuds and parsnips or celeriac), peeled and cut into 4cm chunks

100–150ml hot milk, for thinning—hot full-cream milk is best, as it helps bring all the other hot ingredients together, and you'll end up with a creamier result

120g butter

salt and black pepper

optional extras include mustard, fresh herbs of your choosing, spring onions, nutmeg, and so on

MASHED POTATOES

Method

1. The best spuds for mashing are non-waxy: Pontiac; King Edward; Coliban. Add the potato chunks to a deep pot of cold, salted water, and bring to the boil over high heat. Once boiling, lower the heat and allow to simmer for about 20 minutes or until soft—don't overcook them or you'll end up with mush instead of mash.

2. Drain and return to the pan over very low heat for a couple of minutes to dry them out. Give the pan a good toss so that all the potatoes get their turn on the heat.

3. Remove from the heat and mash well—you want the mix to be as smooth as possible now, before you add the butter and milk. A potato ricer or food mill will give the finest result, but a traditional up and down masher does the job almost as well.

4. Once smooth, tip in the butter first, and mix it in with a wooden spoon, stirring like crazy. Then add just enough milk to bring the mash to a soft, creamy, dropping texture, using a balloon whisk and putting some elbow grease into it. Season to taste with salt and pepper.

5. Add a bit more pizzazz with mustard, herbs, finely chopped spring onions, or nutmeg, if you like.

BAD ROAST POTATOES

Yes, you are probably in a rush and yes you'll lose some of the goodness, but for goodness sake—please peel your potatoes unless you want spuds with the hide of a rhino. Soggy spuds are another no-no, so hold off on the salt until they are cooked. Salt will draw the moisture out and ruin that lovely crisp exterior.

Lastly, don't be tempted to rush the process. There's nothing worse than biting through the crisp skin of a spud only to discover that the interior is still firm, rather than the beautifully soft and fluffy centre you are aiming for.

CHIPS

Crisp and golden on the outside, soft and fluffy as mashed potato on the inside, is it any wonder that the humble fried chip is so irresistible? However, there are a few tricks to getting them just so—particularly for the home cook without access to industrial vats of oil and the other accoutrements of the local fish and chippery:

* Choose the kind of potato that was born to be turned into a chip—Sebago, Russet Burbank, Spunta, King Edward or Bintje are all good. Basically, you can use anything with a floury texture and low moisture content; these hold their shape well and will crisp up beautifully.
* The best chips are those that have been cooked thrice—first parboiled in salted water, then blanched in oil, then fried in oil at a higher temperature.
* As the old saying goes, vegetables that grow in the ground should start off cooking in cold water; vegetables that grow above ground should go into boiling water to cook. So, start your chips off in cold water, please. Parboiling helps soften up and ruffle the edges of the chip, for maximum crispiness when fried.
* Don't overload the chip pan—this will cause the temperature to drop too much and the chips to stick together. Instead, fry them in batches.
* If using a metal chip basket for frying, dip the basket into the hot oil before adding the potatoes—this prevents them from sticking to the metal. A slotted spoon works perfectly well too if you don't have a chip basket handy.
* The first gentle frying process helps dry out the surface of the chips and bind the starches together. At the end of this stage, the chips should be soft, but firm enough to hold their shape during the final frying process.
* The final frying takes place at a higher temperature so that the bonded starchy walls of the chips turn crispy.
* Cooking times can vary with the size of your hob and the variety of potato, so keep a close eye on the colour of your chips when doing the final fry. Aim for golden perfection—not too dark, not too light.

SERVES 4

Ingredients

1kg Sebago potatoes

1.5–2 litres peanut oil (or canola oil), for deep-frying

Method

1. Peel the potatoes and rinse to remove any muddy fingerprints. Cut into slices about 1cm thick, then cut the slices into long chips also about 1cm thick.
2. Add chips to a large pan of salted water. Bring to the boil, then reduce to a gentle simmer (no bubbles) for about 8 minutes.
3. Remove the chips from the water and leave to cool on a cake rack (this helps dry them out). When cool, chill in the fridge—this will also help them crisp up later.

4. In a large heavy-based saucepan, wok or deep-fryer, heat 1.5 litres of oil over medium heat until a small piece of potato skin sizzles when dropped into oil (around 130°C/260°F, if you have a thermometer). Divide the chips into 3 batches.

5. Fry each batch of chips for 5 minutes. Use a slotted spoon to remove the chips to a cake rack (kitchen towel placed underneath will capture the drips). Then repeat with the remaining batches, allowing the oil to reach the right temperature again between batches.

6. Let the chips cool on the rack, then chill in the fridge again.

7. Just before you are ready to eat, heat oil to 190°C (375°F). Again, divide the chips into batches, frying each batch for 2-3 minutes until golden. Remove from the oil with a slotted spoon then spread on a double layer of kitchen towel. Keep the first batches of chips warm in the oven while you bring the oil back up to the right temperature and cook the rest. Serve immediately with plenty of salt.

CHIPS VERSUS CRISPS

To make the other sort of chips, peel 3 large potatoes (or sweet potatoes) and slice very thinly with a mandolin, knife or slicer attachment of a food processor. Place the slices in a bowl, cover with iced water and chill for 1 hour.

Lift from the water and drain on kitchen towel. Heat about 2cm of oil in a deep frying pan to about 190°C (375°F) and fry potato slices in single-layer batches for a minute or 2, or until golden brown and crispy. Lift the chips out with a slotted spoon and drain on kitchen towel.

Sprinkle with salt (and any other seasonings you desire) and serve.

BAD CHIPS

There's a world of difference between a crispy, golden, salty, chip and a limp, soggy, tasteless or pale and undercooked one. You know, the kind that you get from dodgy takeaways, or are served at restaurants and pubs that really should know better.

I put it down to laziness or just plain ignorance. But how hard is it, really, to choose the right kind of spud? To boil water? To plunge the chips into oil? You can even prepare the chips up to the final fry several hours in advance, which takes care of the lack of time argument. So yes, cooking them properly is a bit of a fiddle, but the end result is spectacular.

AVOCADO

Most people know avocados originated in central Mexico. However, you might be surprised to learn that the name comes from the Aztec word *ahuacatl*, meaning testicle. The Aztecs considered the avocado an aphrodisiac, which might explain its prevalence in the modern Mexican diet and the country's high birth rate!

But that's no reason to steer clear of this glorious fruit, which is a member of the laurel family and close cousin to bay and cinnamon trees. A number of varieties are widely available now, each with their own characteristics and growing season. The most common varieties of all are: the Bacon (big and round with a smooth skin); Fuerte (elongated with a textured green skin); Hass (the knobbly purple ones); and the Reed (egg-shaped and super creamy).

To my taste, the best way of eating avocado is with a simple and well-seasoned vinaigrette that allows the star ingredient to shine.

It seems only yesterday when this was a starter that appeared all the time on menus: in that time when avocados were just making their way into people's eating habits.

It truly is one of the great dishes of the world, and so often slaughtered. So here's how to do it right. Gently squeeze your in-season avocado to be sure it's just ripe, and don't decide to continue with the vinaigrette idea until you have sliced and tasted a little piece. The avocado must be perfect in every way.

DRESSED AVOCADO

SERVES 2

Ingredients

2 avocados

120ml walnut oil (or best extra-virgin olive oil at a pinch)

80ml lime juice, freshly squeezed

splash of balsamic vinegar

salt and black pepper

1 chilli, finely sliced

1 tablespoon fresh parsley, finely chopped

toast, finely sliced, to serve

Method

1. Halve the avocados and remove the stone, set the halves aside.
2. Mix together the oil, lime juice and a tiny drop of your best balsamic vinegar. Season with salt and pepper.
3. Add the chilli and parsley, and mix together well. Pour the vinaigrette into the spaces left by the avocado stones.
4. Serve with finely sliced fresh toast, wiped with a little of the dressing.
5. Have some dressing on the side, for replenishment as you work through the flesh.

HOLY GUACAMOLE

Guacamole is a versatile avocado dip that is often served with corn chips and tortillas. It's also used in Mexican cooking as a filling for tacos and a topping for burritos.

Traditionally, guacamole was prepared in a vessel called a *molcajete*, more commonly known today as a mortar and pestle. Simply crush a peeled and de-stoned avocado until soft, then add a finely diced red onion, diced tomato flesh, minced garlic, a couple of finely chopped chillis (depending on your tolerance for heat), lime juice, coriander and a pinch of cumin.

Reed avocados are favoured for this dish as they have naturally higher levels of oil.

BAD AVOCADO

Here are the top four things that will turn a great avocado vinaigrette bad:

* Using poor fruit and believing the dressing will get you through.
* Using slightly overripe or slightly under ripe fruit. To find out if an avocado is perfectly ripe, press it gently with your thumb. It should not feel mushy or soft, but should give just a little. If you want to speed up the ripening process of unripe avocados, place them together in a paper bag and leave in a sunny spot for a day or two. Or nestle them next to a ripe banana—the gases given off help speed up the ripening process.
* Using a shop-bought, commercially made dressing, or worse, believing that the vinegar/acid is the flavouring tool, not the beautiful oil. These make for puckered lips and no trace of avocado flavour.
* With a core ingredient that is this good, you don't need to hide it within a salad, or serve alongside a protein, such as chopped chicken, ham, seafood, or anything really: this is about the delicious flesh of the fruit shining through.

ZUCCHINI

Fancy the swollen ovary of a flower, anyone? That's essentially what you are eating every time you tuck into a zucchini (or courgette).

As anyone who has ever taken their eye off the veggie patch for a few minutes can testify, zucchini can grow up to three metres in length, but are generally tough and stringy once they reach this stage. If you want to eat them—rather than deploying them as funky light sabres—go for the young ones (under 20cm in length).

These have tender skin, soft seeds, and a delicate flavour that needs nothing more than a quick tumble in some seasoned butter or olive oil, with or without some snipped fresh herbs.

As a delicately flavoured vegetable—more correctly, the immature fruit of the zucchini plant—zucchini work equally well in savoury and sweet dishes, such as cakes. Even the flowers can be stuffed and deep-fried—kind of like a floral tempura.

ZUCCHINI, LEMON AND FETA FRITTERS

MAKES 8-10 FRITTERS (SERVES 4-5 PEOPLE AS PART OF A SPREAD; 2-3 AS A MAIN DISH)

Ingredients

zest and juice of 1 lemon, plus wedges to serve

4 large zucchinis, grated

2 eggs

2 tablespoons plain flour

pinch of dried chilli

½ bunch fresh mint, finely chopped

pinch of dried oregano

150g feta, crumbled

salt and black pepper

olive oil, for shallow-frying

lemon wedges and salad, to serve

Method

1. Zest 1 lemon then squeeze the juice into a large bowl. Add the grated zucchinis and mix well.

2. Whisk the eggs in a separate bowl, and add to the zucchini mix, along with the flour, chilli, mint, oregano and feta.

3. Mix well and season with salt and pepper, taking into account that feta can be quite salty.

4. When ready to cook, add a good couple of slugs of olive oil to 2 frying pans and put 4-5 spoonfuls of the mixture into each, to make 8-10 fritters. Cook until golden underneath, then flip and continue cooking until golden all over.

5. Serve with lemon wedges and salad. Or, if you plan to serve them cold as part of a picnic spread, remember to pack fresh pitta bread and olives.

OTHER WAYS WITH ZUCCHINI

The humble zucchini is supremely versatile and lends itself to an array of dishes due to its ability to take on the flavours of the ingredients it is prepared with. In addition, the method of cooking also has a significant impact. Here are some ideas to take your zucchini skills to the next level:

* Impart a charred, smoky flavour by barbecuing or chargrilling chunks of zucchini as part of a veggie kebab.
* Grate it and toss thin discs of slivers of zucchini through fresh pasta.
* Cubes of zucchini taste great when grilled on top of a homemade pizza (see page 40)
* Try making a sweet loaf of zucchini and banana bread (think carrot cake, if you need some help to get over the vegetable/fruit weirdness factor).
* Hollow out a whole zucchini and stuff it with bolognese (see page 80), drizzle with cheese sauce (see page 84) and pop it into the oven to bake. Great comfort food!
* Shred raw zucchini into a salad for added colour and bite.
* Fling chunks of the vegetable into a *ratatouille*—a vegetarian French stew (tomatoes are a key ingredient, as well as eggplant and capsicums) that is sautéed in olive oil and then cooked slowly in the oven over a very long time.

BAD ZUCCHINI

Once upon a time, zucchini was simply sliced into rounds and boiled. The result? Grey discs of slime, with little nutritional value and even less flavour. Thankfully, the cucumber hybrid is today treated with respect and is regularly served steamed, boiled, grilled, stuffed and baked, barbecued and fried. It is also a good source of Vitamin C and B6, riboflavin and manganese. It is hard to go too wrong; just remember its delicate flavour and fleshy middle need to be treated with care.

VEGETABLE SALAD

Less a salad than an all-in-one kind of meal, this dish is inspired by the Indonesian dish *gado gado*, and made with loads of veggies cooked very lightly and served with a tangy satay sauce. In Indonesian, *gado gado* means medley or mix, which is exactly what this dish is, and it's served everywhere from posh restaurants to street stalls. These humble food outlets are known as *kaki lima*, which literally translates to 'five feet'—refering to the vendor's two feet and the cart's two wheels in the front and one supporting leg at the back.

Perfect for hot weather, it's light and refreshing, while also having enough body from the potatoes and peanut dressing to fill the hungriest of stomachs.

Traditionally it is served topped with prawn crackers, so you get the contrast between the cooked vegetables and the crunch of the crackers. Be careful to add these only at the last minute though, or else they'll go soggy, which defeats the whole purpose. For a more filling meal, serve with rice. Chilli, shrimp and tamarind pastes and palm sugar are available at Asian supermarkets.

SERVES 6

Ingredients

For the satay sauce

150g roasted, unsalted peanuts (skinned)

2 tablespoons peanut oil

2 shallots, finely chopped

2 garlic cloves, crushed

2 teaspoons chilli paste

2 teaspoons shrimp paste

2 teaspoons finely grated palm sugar or brown sugar, plus extra to taste

2 tablespoons tamarind paste

1 tablespoon lime juice

270ml can coconut milk

Method

1. First, make the satay sauce. Finely grind the peanuts in a food processor. Heat the oil in a deep frying pan over low to medium heat. Add the chopped shallots and garlic, and cook for 3-4 minutes until the onion is soft.

2. Stir in the ground peanuts, chilli and shrimp pastes, sugar, tamarind paste, lime juice, coconut milk and 1 cup water. Mix well, bring to the boil, then reduce the heat to low and simmer for 10 minutes or until thickened. Taste and season accordingly with a little more salt and sugar. Keep it somewhere warm while you assemble the salad.

3. Blanch the beans (4 minutes), cabbage (1 minute), choy sum (1 minute) and bean sprouts (30 seconds) in boiling salted water until just tender. Refresh briefly in cold water, then drain well.

4. Gently toss with the cucumber, eggs, potatoes, tofu and coriander leaves, and serve drizzled with some of the warm satay sauce. Sprinkle with a few deep-fried shallots too, if you like.

VEGETABLE SALAD

For the salad

200g snake or green beans, cut into 4cm lengths

200g Chinese cabbage, shredded

250g choy sum, roughly chopped

250g bean sprouts

½ medium cucumber, thickly sliced

4 hard-boiled free-range eggs, peeled, halved

2 peeled potatoes, boiled in water coloured with a teaspoon of tumeric, diced

100g firm tofu, cut into 1cm thick slices

3 tablespoons fresh coriander leaves

deep-fried shallots (available from Asian supermarkets)

prawn crackers, to serve

RINGING THE CHANGES

All sorts of veggies can be tossed into a salad like this—in its country of origin, Indonesia, you might also find young jackfruit or bitter melon (peeled and cooked), lettuce or fried *tempeh* (a high protein, fermented soybean product) rather than tofu. Steer clear of carrots and tomatoes though—these are definitely not authentic.

You can also make the sauce with cashew nuts rather than peanuts, just so long as they are unsalted and lightly toasted.

For a more Australian take on the vegetable salad, throw chunks of potatoes, sweet potatoes, pumpkins and/or squashes, zucchini and onions onto a baking tray or roasting tin and splash with olive oil and balsamic vinegar.

Roast in a 200°C (400°F) oven until the vegetables are tender and browned.

BAD VEGETABLE SALAD

In a word, overcooked. The vegetables for this need to be cooked very lightly in water, not boiled to a mush. You want some crunch—not too much and not too little. To make sure they get exactly the right amount of time, cook them separately and use a timer or keep a careful eye on your watch. Taste them to check—don't rely upon sight alone.

PASTA AND NOODLES

HOMEMADE PASTA 76
SHOP-BOUGHT PASTA 78
BOLOGNESE 80
GNOCCHI 82
MACARONI CHEESE 84

CHAPTER 5

PASTA AND NOODLES

Remember the days when canned spaghetti was considered exotic? Or noodles only came in a packet with freeze-dried flavourings? My, we've come a long way.

Pasta and noodles are now everyday staples, mainly because they are easy to cook, but also because they carry flavours so well. Think about how a rich tomato sauce blankets a twirl of pasta, or how noodles snuggle around stir-fried veggies, and are coated in liquid at the same time. Carriers, both of them. Like any trusted servant, they should be treated well…

HOMEMADE PASTA

With a little practice, it's easy to make fresh pasta that knocks the socks off anything from a packet. The dough is made from a mix of eggs and flour, ideally '00' high-gluten flour, which is kneaded like bread dough and then pressed through the rollers of a pasta machine until thin and glossy. Then it's cut into long strings or ribbons, or formed and stuffed to make tortellini or ravioli.

Because it contains eggs and additional water, fresh pasta is more tender than dried and takes about half the time to cook. Its delicate texture is best suited to accompany light sauces made with tomatoes, cream, olive oil, or butter flavoured with a mixture of dry, but preferably fresh, herbs.

The only drawback to making your own pasta is the fact that you need to invest in a pasta machine—but heck, think of it as a lifetime investment in good eating. And you will soon recoup your expenses when you start making up large batches of fresh pasta to freeze for a quick dinner.

But if you are determined to save your cents, and feel like mastering a recipe that doubles up as an exercise routine, you can simply use a rolling pin and cut the dough into ribbons with a sharp knife, but be warned—you might not have the energy left to lift the cooked pasta to your mouth.

MAKES ABOUT 900 GRAMS

Ingredients

550g '00' flour
(or a mix of '00' flour and semolina)

1 teaspoon fine salt

4 large free-range eggs, plus 3 extra yolks, lightly beaten

1 tablespoon olive oil

Method

1. Tip the flour and salt onto a clean work surface and shape into a volcano. Make a well in the middle, and pour in two-thirds of the eggs and the olive oil.

2. Using your fingertips, gradually bring the flour into the liquid until you have a dough you can bring together in a ball, adding more egg if necessary.

3. To knead the dough, push it away from you with the heel of your hand, then roll it back on itself towards you so it folds in half. Push it away again, and continue the process for about 10 minutes until it is smooth and matt. You'll know it's ready when it springs back when poked.

4. Divide into 2 balls, wrap in clingfilm and allow to rest for about an hour in the fridge—the longer the better, even overnight if you can.

5. Roll out the first ball of dough on a lightly floured surface until it is about 1cm thick and will easily go through the widest setting of your pasta machine.

6. Sprinkle with flour and roll through the pasta machine over and over again until it's very thin, smooth and even. (Machines vary, but the instructions will probably tell you to work down from the highest setting to the lowest as you go). Or you can do it by hand with a rolling pin.

7. When the pasta is shiny and thin enough for your liking, cut using a knife or the cutter on your pasta machine. Curl into portion-sized nests and leave on a floured surface, under a damp cloth, while you repeat with the rest of the dough.

8. Bring a large pan of well-salted water to the boil, add the pasta, in batches if necessary, and cook for a couple of minutes, stirring occasionally to keep it moving. Serve immediately.

THE FINISHING TOUCH

After all your hard work making the pasta, I wouldn't go overboard when it comes to the sauce. Try warming some cream with a sharp blue cheese, make a proper carbonara (that means no cream!), or even toss the pasta with some fresh spring vegetables, steamed or lightly cooked in oil until just *al dente*.

My other store cupboard favourite is spicy and tangy *sugo alla puttanesca*. Literally meaning 'whore's-style sauce' in Italian, it is supposedly named because it's ready in the time it takes a lady of the night to look after a client.

For this, simply fry up a few garlic cloves and a big pinch of dried chilli, toss in a cup of chopped black olives, eight chopped anchovies and a tin of diced tomatoes, and cook until thick and fragrant.

Mix together with the hot, cooked pasta, and serve with freshly chopped parsley and grated parmesan.

BAD HOMEMADE PASTA

Like bread dough, pasta dough needs to be treated with respect. So don't leave it sitting around in the open air, or it will get dry and crusty.

Tough pasta is the result of not kneading for long enough—don't skimp on this step as the kneading process stretches the gluten in the dough so that the end result is light and silky.

Resting in the fridge is also important as it will be too elastic and springy to roll when you first bring it together into a dough.

SHOP-BOUGHT PASTA

As simple as it might sound to grab a packet of dried pasta from the pantry and tip it into a saucepan of boiling water, there are a couple of tricks to cooking it perfectly each and every time.

Firstly, the water needs to be at a rolling boil before you add the pasta, so that it starts cooking straight away and doesn't just bob about in the water waiting for it to get up to speed.

To check if the water is ready, bring it to the boil then fling in a pinch of table or sea salt—if the water surges around the salt, you're okay to add the pasta.

Secondly, once the pasta is in, you need to cover the pot to bring the water back to the boil. Once it has reached the rolling boil stage again, remove the lid and give the pasta a good stir. It is important to do this often to stop the pasta clumping together—this is certainly not the effect you are looking for and will result in uneven cooking.

Some people solve the problem by adding a few tablespoons of white vinegar to the boiling water, as this makes the pasta less sticky and reduces some of its starch. But as long as you keep stirring, you should be fine.

The instructions on the packet are there for a reason, so follow them and all should go to plan. Be aware that different types of pasta take different times to cook, depending on their size and whether they're made of wholemeal grains, the normal yellow durum wheat, or even spelt.

It's always worth checking during the cooking time just in case—which is where the phrase *al dente* comes in. Essentially this means 'to the tooth'—so the pasta should be tender but still have a bite to it.

The recipe given below is about as simple as it gets—a handful of pantry ingredients, plus some parsley from the garden or balcony and whatever pasta you have to hand.

SERVES 4

Ingredients

500g pasta

¼ cup olive oil

2 tablespoons lemon zest, shredded

2 tablespoons salted capers, rinsed

1 cup fresh parsley leaves

1 teaspoon chilli flakes

grated parmesan, to serve

PASTA WITH CRISPY PARSLEY

Method

1. Cook the pasta in a big saucepan of boiling, salted water until *al dente*.
2. When the pasta is just about ready, heat the oil over medium heat and gently fry the lemon, capers, parsley and chilli until the parsley is crisp.
3. Toss through the hot pasta and serve with grated parmesan as a simple meal or side dish.

TYPES OF PASTA

Italy is home to a vast array of pasta shapes, some are only found in specific regions, while others have been embraced around the world. Here are a few basic varieties to get you started:

* Long-form string pasta—anything spaghetti-like that you can twist around your fork. These pastas are made in varying widths, from the thinnest type—angel hair (*capelli d'angelo*)—to the thicker vermicelli and, at the even plumper end of the scale, bucatini. They can be either solid or hollow, like bucatini.
* Long-form ribbon pasta—these varieties are flat and come in varying widths, think fettuccine, lasagne, linguine and tagliatelle.
* Tubular pasta—can be tiny or jumbo-sized, smooth or ridged (*rigati*), straight-cut or diagonally cut. Elbows (most often used in macaroni cheese, see page 84), manicotti (large enough to be stuffed with a variety of fillings), penne and rigatoni are well-known types.
* Shaped pasta—there are hundreds of ways to twist, curl or shape pasta, but you're most likely to find the following kinds in your local supermarket—farfalle (bow ties), fusilli (corkscrews), ruote (wagon wheels). These varieties are great if you want the sauce to really cling to your pasta.
* Pre-stuffed pasta—this group includes agnolotti and mezzelune (semicircular pockets), ravioli and tortellini.
* Irregular shaped pasta—includes 'dumpling' pastas like gnocchi, which is usually round in shape and made with flour plus potatoes (see page 82).

BAD PASTA

When it comes to cooking pasta, timing is absolutely everything. *Al dente* pasta is toothsome, but pasta that has been undercooked is more likely to be crunchy and inedible.

You should also be very wary of overcooking pasta as it becomes incredibly glutinous and slimy. The end result? A plateful of mush. Check the instructions on the packet, keep checking the texture of the pasta as you stir and, if need be, set a timer.

BOLOGNESE

Named after its birthplace in Bologna in Italy, there's perhaps no other pasta dish that screams Italian more than spaghetti bolognese. Funnily enough for such an iconic dish, there's no definitive recipe, with all sorts of versions turning up, even in its native Italy.

The meat-based tomato sauce is simply referred to as *ragù* in its home city, but as chefs and home cooks all over the world fell for the rustic charms of bolognese, a proliferation of additions, variations and substitutions have come to pass.

Here are just some of the ingredients that people battle over: cream or milk; the addition of garlic and mushrooms; minced beef, veal, pork or even sausage; pancetta, bacon or cured ham; tomato paste or whole canned tomatoes; fresh tomatoes or passata; red or white wine, or no wine at all.

Chicken liver is another more debatable addition—this adds richness, but probably isn't worth the bother unless you have a ready supply.

For a perfectly tender and meaty stew, it needs to be rich in tomato, garlic and olive oil, and cooked long and slow on the stovetop or in a very low oven if you're worried about the bottom catching.

Serve with homemade gnocchi (see page 82) or any kind of pasta you fancy—tagliatelle is the popular choice in Italy—and you'll find recipes for homemade and shop-bought pasta on pages 76 and 78.

It is always worth freezing any extra sauce for a speedy week-night dinner, simply defrost, heat in a casserole dish and cook your pasta from scratch.

SERVES 4

Ingredients

3 tablespoons olive oil

100g smoked streaky bacon or pancetta, finely diced

1 onion, finely diced

3 garlic cloves, crushed

1 carrot, finely diced

1 stick celery, finely diced

300g beef mince, at room temperature

salt and black pepper

Method

1. Preheat oven to 120°C (250°F).

2. Warm the olive oil in a large heavy-based casserole dish over gentle heat, and then add the bacon. Once the bacon fat has started to melt, add the onion and cover. Cook gently for about 15 minutes until golden and translucent.

3. Tip in the garlic, carrot and celery and cook for a further 5-10 minutes.

4. Crumble the beef into the dish and allow to brown for about 10 minutes, using a wooden spoon to break up any lumps. The meat should have completely lost its red colour.

5. Season well with salt and pepper, then stir in the chopped liver (if using), and let it cook for another 5 minutes.

| 40g chicken liver, finely chopped (optional) |
| 150ml dry white wine |
| handful of fresh herbs—thyme, marjoram, oregano, for example |
| 2 bay leaves |
| 1 can (400g) plum tomatoes |
| pasta—spaghetti, tagliatelle, for example—or gnocchi |
| grated parmesan or pecorino cheese, to serve |

6. Tip in the wine, herbs, bay leaves and the tomatoes, and stir well. The meat needs to be almost covered with liquid during the first hour to prevent it drying out.

7. Pop the casserole into the oven, with the lid slightly ajar, and cook for at least 3 hours or until the meat is very tender. Take an occasional peek, and top up with a little water or wine if it seems too dry.

8. Fish out the bay leaves and serve with pasta or gnocchi, and grated parmesan or pecorino cheese.

TAKE IT ONE STEP FURTHER WITH A LASAGNE OR MOUSSAKA

Having perfected bolognese sauce, here's how to turn it into lasagne. All you need are some lasagne sheets (fresh is best if you can get them), one quantity of sauce (refer to the recipe on the left) and one quantity of béchamel sauce (see page 130). Oh, and a bit of freshly grated parmesan or pecorino to ensure you get a nicely browned top layer.

Lightly grease an ovenproof dish with butter, and put a layer of lasagne sheets on the bottom. Cover with a layer of the meat sauce, then a layer of the béchamel sauce. Sprinkle with the cheese, then repeat the layers of pasta and sauces until all the ingredients have been used up—be sure to finish with a layer of béchamel and give this an extra sprinkling of parmesan or pecorino. Bake in a 200°C (400°F) oven for 30 minutes or until golden and bubbling.

The classic Greek dish of *moussaka* is made in much the same way, except the layers of pasta (the lasagne sheets) are replaced with layers of sliced and fried eggplant (see page 63).

BAD BOLOGNESE

This usually occurs when the dish hasn't been cooked long enough. You really need hours and hours of slow, gloopy simmering in the oven to get the right richness—simply frying up some beef mince and adding tomato paste won't do, despite generations of university students believing otherwise.

GNOCCHI

Like much Italian peasant food (pizza included), gnocchi is based around a couple of staple ingredients—potatoes and flour—and was originally designed to fill an empty stomach after a hard day's work in the fields. You can add an egg to your list of ingredients if you're worried about your gorgeous, tender gnocchi falling apart when they hit the water.

The main thing with gnocchi is to use the right kind of spud. That means something that's old and floury, and kind of dry. Those old Desiree potatoes in the back of your pantry are perfect. Young or waxy spuds have a much higher water content, which means you'll need more flour to bring the dough together, and this will make your gnocchi heavier.

Some recipes swear by baking the spuds, then mashing the cooked flesh, but boiling them works just as well if you follow the other instructions to the letter. And preparing them doesn't take as long as you might think. A bit like making bread (see page 180), you'll soon get into the rhythm.

SERVES 4

Ingredients

750g Desiree potatoes, unpeeled

pinch of salt

200g plain flour, plus a little extra for rolling

Method

1. Boil the potatoes in their skins for 20-25 minutes or until just tender when tested with a skewer. Drain well, and when cool enough to handle, rip the skins off by hand and discard.

2. Purée the spuds with a potato ricer (or mouli or food processor, depending on how well kitted out your kitchen is). Season to taste with salt.

3. On a floured surface, tip out the potatoes, add most of the flour and then use your hands to knead briefly until a soft dough forms. If mixture is still sticky, add a little more of the flour.

4. Using your hands, roll the dough into long thin logs, about 2cm in diameter. Cut each log into 1.5cm long pieces.

5. If you want to get fancy, you can then roll each ball of gnocchi over the tines of a lightly floured fork, to form a dent in the back of each one and fork marks on the other side (this puts crinkles in the surface, which will help your sauce cling to the cooked gnocchi).

6. To cook the gnocchi, bring a large saucepan of water to the boil. Add about a ¼ of the gnocchi and allow to cook until they float to the surface of the water.
7. Continue cooking gnocchi at the surface for about 10 seconds then remove with a large slotted spoon and drain well. Repeat with remaining gnocchi. Serve immediately with your favourite sauce.

SIMPLE SAUCES

Having spent so much time creating perfect gnocchi, give yourself a break with one of these very simple, very quick sauces:

★ Sage and burnt butter sauce: Brown some butter in a frying pan, adding fresh sage once the butter is melted and bubbling. Toss in the gnocchi and allow them to brown lightly in some spots. Season with salt, pepper and lemon juice, and sprinkle with grated parmesan.

★ Tomato, garlic, chilli and basil sauce: Heat some olive oil in a frying pan, add chopped garlic, and cook until fragrant. Then add tinned or fresh tomatoes, seeded and chopped, to the pan and bring to a simmer. Season with salt and stir in the fresh basil and dried or fresh chilli to taste. Cook until the basil has just given up the ghost, then toss with the cooked gnocchi.

★ Gnocchi and cheese sauce: Place the cooked gnocchi in a buttered casserole dish, dot with butter, and sprinkle grated parmesan and/or fontina cheese on top. Grill until cheese is melted and starting to brown.

BAD GNOCCHI

Done well, gnocchi are tender, light little pillows—done badly, they're heavy, dense dumplings that could do serious duty in a pinball machine. There are generally four reasons why you might end up with the second sort.

First, you've used the wrong kind of spud (see above). Second, the potato hasn't been mashed finely enough. An ordinary masher isn't up to this task—you really need a mouli or potato ricer (kind of like a garlic press, but designed to turn your boiled spuds into the clouds of light mash).

Third, you've mucked up the balance of flour: too much will make the cooked gnocchi tough; too little, and the gnocchi will disintegrate during cooking. Fourth and finally, you've spent too long playing with the dough and it's now more like play dough than something you want to put in your mouth. No amount of sauce is going to disguise the fact that you've screwed up.

MACARONI CHEESE

This classic comfort food dish has been around for years, with the first written mention of a pasta and cheese casserole cropping up in the medieval Italian cookbook, *Liber de Coquina*. Since sweeping across Europe, the humble 'mac and cheese' was adopted stateside, when Thomas Jefferson discovered the dish in Paris and decided to serve it up at an 1802 state dinner.

While carbs and dairy are the dieter's nightmare, they are also the really hungry or greedy person's delight. And few dishes fit the bill better than macaroni and cheese in all its gooey, cheesy splendour.

This is the kind of dish that anyone over the age of 10 should be able to cook—the kind of dish that can be rustled up from a couple of pantry and fridge staples.

Just make sure that the pasta is cooked *al dente* (just undercooked so that it's soft on the outside but firm in the centre) and that the sauce is suitably cheesy. You should also cook it in a large, flat dish rather than a deeper smaller one, as it is the contrast between the crunchy topping and the meltingly smooth pasta underneath that most people lust after.

You can make macaroni and cheese via the method below, but if you have any leftover white sauce (see page 130) then simply toss in the cheese, cooked onion and macaroni and you're away. Hell, any type of pasta works here. The smaller the better though, as you want the sauce to ooze into as many nooks and crannies as possible.

SERVES 4

Ingredients

½ cup butter

1 onion, finely chopped

½ cup bacon, chopped (optional)

3 tablespoons plain flour

2 cups full-cream milk

1 tablespoon wholegrain mustard (optional)

1½ cups grated tasty cheese

225g macaroni (cooked in a large pan of salted water according to packet instructions and drained)

salt and black pepper

½ cup breadcrumbs (dried for preference and convenience)

Method

1. Melt the butter in a pan and gently cook the onion (and bacon, if using) for about 5 minutes until soft. Stir in the flour and cook briefly, making sure it doesn't catch. Add the milk and stir constantly until the sauce boils and thickens.

2. Remove from heat and stir in the mustard (if using) and most of the cheese. Season to taste.

3. Mix the pasta with the sauce and place in a greased ovenproof dish. Sprinkle with breadcrumbs and remaining cheese and bake in a 180°C (350°F) oven for about 15 minutes or until the top is golden and bubbling.

COMFORT FOODS

Funnily enough, the term 'comfort food' has only been around since 1977 according to Webster's Dictionary, where it is defined as: "Food prepared in a traditional style having a usually nostalgic or sentimental appeal." But the idea of dishes that are cherished for the memories they hold has been around far longer.

Generally easy-to-eat and easy-to-digest, comfort foods are as varied as our national cuisines. While the English might reach for a rich and creamy rice pudding or hearty serving of bangers and mash (mashed potatoes and sausages), across the Atlantic, the ultimate feel-good grub includes Southern-fried chicken and grilled cheese sandwiches.

Australians tend to reach for a lamb-filled pie or a hefty chunk of coconut-sprinkled lamington. Other comfort foods include *lihapiirakka* (a meat doughnut) in Finland, *laksa* (spicy noodle soup) in Malaysia, croissants for the French, *nasi goreng* (a fried rice dish eaten for breakfast) in Indonesia, *kim chi* (fermented vegetables) in Korea and miso soup in Japan.

BAD MACARONI AND CHEESE

In a word: packet. This fluorescent orange dish, made from chemicals resembling nothing found in nature, may be a winner with kids and impoverished students, but is unlikely to find favour with anyone over the age of 5 or not under the influence.

If making it yourself, you can also ruin this simple dish with a couple of beginner mistakes—overcooking the pasta to sogginess, undercooking it so that you risk your teeth with every bite, or allowing the sauce to catch and burn. You also need to be judicious with your use of sauce—just enough to cling to the pasta and hold it together, not enough to drown it in a cheesy soup.

RICE AND GRAINS

RISOTTO 88
COUSCOUS 90
TABOULI 92
QUINOA 94

CHAPTER 6

RICE AND GRAINS

Simple and unassuming they may be, but rices and grains offer an almost dizzying variety of uses. Being cheap and long lasting as well, the ability to cook a few perfect dishes based on these pantry staples is a skill well worth mastering.

Essentially, all you're doing here is rehydrating the dried grains (whether rice, couscous or whatever) so that they're tender to eat and more digestible. Sometimes you want a little crunch left, like with the burghul in tabouli (see page 92); other times, you're aiming for creamy smoothness, like with the grains of rice in risotto (see page 88). The simplest way is to swell the grains in water, but using stock, or a mixture of stock and wine or other liquid, will add extra punch to the finished dish. Many of the grains can be swapped for each other too—think of using herbed quinoa to accompany a curry instead of rice.

RISOTTO

Good risotto starts with good starchy rice—Arborio for example, Vialone Nano or perhaps Carnaroli. Then it's all in the cooking. First is the step known as *tostatura*, where the rice and onions are toasted in oil or butter so that the grains are completely coated.

It's important that neither are allowed to brown—the onions, because they'll ruin the flavour of the finished dish, and the rice, because this locks in the starch that you need for the creamy texture. Ensure the wine is absorbed. Only then do you start adding ladlefuls of stock. You need to stir all the while. This helps to release the starch from the grains.

At its most basic, risotto can be a simple mix of rice and cheese, and perhaps a few freshly snipped herbs, but it's also the perfect vehicle for carrying other flavours, too—the meat from a slow-cooked ox tail, a handful of podded peas, sugar peas or green beans, roasted capsicums, olives and cheese, or even puréed pumpkin and smoked bacon. At what stage you add the ingredients will depend on what you're adding—cooked meat can be stirred in at the last minute, just so that it heats through, or vegetables can be cooked in the stock along with the rice.

If using bacon or pancetta, I'd fry this at the same time as the onions and rice.

After 15 minutes or so, your risotto will be approaching perfection—smooth, rich, creamy and just *al dente* to the bite. Grab a spoon and have a taste. It's much better to test it too often than to find out you have a soggy, overcooked mess, or an undercooked bunch of crunchy grains.

Now it's time for the *mantecato* stage, where more butter and grated cheese is beaten into the risotto, and it's allowed to rest for several minutes. It's worth making time for this, no matter how hungry you are, as it gives the rice time to relax into a glossy mess, not quite liquid, but not quite solid either—*all'onda*, as the Italians would describe it.

RISOTTO

SERVES 2

Ingredients

1 tablespoon butter or olive oil

½ onion, finely chopped

1 clove garlic, finely chopped

200g Carnaroli rice

1 small glass white wine

1¼ litres good stock, chicken or vegetable, almost boiling

50g unsalted butter, diced, for finishing

50g parmesan, grated

Method

1. In a heavy-based pan, melt the butter or heat the oil and soften the onion and garlic. Toss in the rice and stir it around on low heat for a couple of minutes, so that the grains are coated in the butter or oil.

2. When the rice is hot, slosh in the wine, and keep stirring until this has evaporated. Then you're ready to start adding the stock, a ladleful at a time. Stir until it has nearly all been absorbed—the rice should always be sloppy, rather than dry—and then add another ladleful, and so on.

3. Add any extra ingredients at some point during this time, depending on how robust they are, usually about 10 minutes in.

4. When the rice begins to soften (after about 13 minutes, but the only way to know is to keep checking), add the stock in smaller amounts, and test it regularly, until it is cooked to your liking. Then add 50g of diced butter and 50g of grated cheese, and beat like mad, until the risotto is rich and creamy. Check seasoning and serve.

EASY ARANCINI

This is a great way of using up any leftover risotto. Simply mix 3 cups of risotto with 1 egg, lightly beaten, and add some extra flavourings if you wish (a sprinkling of chilli flakes, crushed garlic, zest of 1 lemon, mixed herbs, and so on). Form the mixture into small balls, roll in flour and set aside. Then simply heat some oil in a wok or deep-fryer, and cook in batches until golden brown.

Remove from the oil with a slotted spoon, drain on kitchen towel and keep warm in a hot oven while you finishing cooking the rest.

BAD RISOTTO

Risotto is one of those dishes that should be quick, simple and delicious, but is actually very easy to get very wrong. It's important to use the best stock you can make or get your hands on—a watery stock will lead to a distinct lack of flavour in the finished dish. The stock needs to be piping hot too, or you'll waste precious time waiting for it to heat up, and all the while your rice is overcooking.

A final word of warning: if you don't want to end up with food poisoning, make sure that any pre-cooked meats you add to your risotto are heated through very well first.

RICE AND GRAINS

COUSCOUS

Couscous is a type of semolina made from wheat grain, and is a great alternative to rice, pasta, potatoes and other carbohydrates. A staple dish in North Africa for more than a thousand years, traditionally couscous is cooked in a steamer basket over a stew or broth.

Today, the couscous you'll find in the supermarket is generally of the instant variety. To cook it, all you have to do is place the couscous in a large bowl, pour over some hot liquid (water or stock), and let it sit until the grains have swollen. Season well, then rake it around with a fork to break up any lumps. The end result should be extremely light, with each grain soft and velvety but separate from its neighbor—not a stodgy porridge.

By itself, couscous tastes rather bland. Just like rice, it gets its flavour from whatever it is served with, although you can also punch up the taste by adding toasted pine nuts, almonds, sultanas or herbs such as oregano, thyme, basil or spices before adding the boiling liquid. You can also add more flavour by substituting beef, chicken, fish or vegetable stock for the boiling water, as in the recipe here. This works brilliantly as a side dish with fish (see page 100) or a slow-cooked meat (see page 116), or as part of a barbecue spread.

Any dish served with couscous is traditionally accompanied by a fiery sauce made with the juices of the stew or some of the broth, sparked up with chilli, cayenne pepper or harissa (a concentrated paste of red pimento).

CARAMELISED ONION COUSCOUS

SERVES XX

Ingredients

2 tablespoons olive oil or butter

2 red onions, thinly sliced

2 garlic cloves, crushed

¼ cup red wine vinegar

salt and black pepper

1½ cups chicken or vegetable stock

2 teaspoons harissa paste

1½ cups couscous

¼ cup currants

Method

1. Heat 1 tablespoon of olive oil in a frying pan over medium heat. Cook the onion and garlic, stirring every so often, for 10-15 minutes or until golden and lightly caramelised. Add vinegar and cook, stirring, for a couple of minutes. Season with salt and pepper and allow to cool.

2. Heat the stock over medium heat. Add the harissa and whisk to combine.

3. Place the couscous in a large bowl with a teaspoon of sea salt and pour over the hot stock and harissa mix. Cover and let stand for 10 minutes.

400g can chickpeas,
rinsed and drained

juice of 1 lemon,
plus wedges to serve

1 long red chilli,
seeds removed, finely chopped

1 cup fresh flat-leaf parsley leaves,
finely chopped

2 cups fresh mint leaves,
1 cup should be finely chopped,
the other left whole

4. Fluff the couscous with a fork so that there are no lumps, then stir through the onion, currants, chickpeas, lemon juice, chilli, parsley and the chopped and whole mint leaves (reserving a few as a garnish).

5. Add a tablespoon of olive oil, taste for seasoning and stir once more. Serve warm or cold.

GOING NUTTY

To give plain couscous a rich, nutty flavour, heat 4 tablespoons of olive oil in a saucepan. Add 2 cups of couscous and a good shake of salt to the hot oil. Cook for several minutes, stirring constantly to prevent burning, until the couscous is golden. Then add 2½ cups of boiling water.

Remove from the heat and cover. Let the couscous sit until all the water is absorbed and the grains are soft, about 5 minutes, then loosen the couscous with a fork and serve.

For an even more nutty flavour and added crunch, stir in ¼ cup of toasted pine nuts alongside the onion, currants and chickpeas.

Roughly chopped pecans or almonds also work well and give the dish more texture, but these additions are not as traditional. The nuts also add an extra burst of protein to this already high-protein grain, which also boasts higher levels of riboflavin, niacin, Vitamin B6, and folate when compared to pasta.

BAD COUSCOUS

Couscous is meant to be fluffy, not mushy, so be careful to use the right quantity of liquid.

It's best to be on the stingy side, as you can always add more. Adding too much liquid, and adding it too quickly, will result in a glutinous mess that could be used to hang wallpaper. Not appealing. Always read the instructions on the packet—unlike pasta, couscous soaks up all the water it's 'cooked' in and, if left even a little too long, will become sticky.

TABOULI

Great tabouli should sing in your mouth with an explosion of lemon, mint, parsley and onion. Brilliant with roasted meats—particularly lamb—it's also a natural partner to hummus (a dip made from cooked and mashed chickpeas, blended with tahini, olive oil, lemon juice, salt and garlic), falafel and other flavourful and aromatic Middle Eastern dishes.

For such a moist and fresh salad, you might be surprised to learn that the trick lies in keeping each of the ingredients dry until they are all brought together with the zingy lemon-spiked dressing.

Herbs should be washed then either spun in a salad spinner or wrapped in a tea towel and whipped around your head so that all the drops of water fly out.

The bulgur (cracked wheat) is also soaked, to make it swell, then drained and allowed to dry so that the grains are distinct and combine easily with the other ingredients.

It is also possible to use couscous (see page 90) or quinoa (see page 94) in a tabouli if you don't have any bulgur to hand.

SERVES 6

Ingredients

60g bulgur (cracked wheat)

juice of 2 lemons

100ml olive oil

sea salt and black pepper

3 medium tomatoes, seeds removed and finely chopped

250g spring onions, ends trimmed, finely chopped

4 cups (loosely packed) fresh flat-leaf parsley, washed, dried and finely chopped

1 cup (loosely packed) fresh mint, washed, dried and finely chopped

Method

1. Place the bulgur in a medium bowl. Add enough cold water to cover and set aside for 1 hour to soak.

2. Drain bulgur through a fine sieve and use your hands to squeeze out any excess moisture. Spread bulgur over a baking tray lined with kitchen towel and set aside for 30 minutes to dry.

3. Combine the lemon juice and olive oil in a screw-top jar. Season with sea salt flakes and pepper. Shake until well combined.

4. Combine the bulgur, tomato, spring onions, parsley and mint in a large serving bowl. Drizzle with the dressing and stir to combine. Serve immediately.

MARVELLOUS MEZE

In many parts of the Mediterranean and the Middle East, tabouli is often served as part of a delicious spread of small dishes known as meze or mezze.

Other popular dishes include the chickpea-based dip, hummus, usually served with toasted pita bread, *kibbe* (meatballs made with burgul, spiced minced meat and herbs), grilled or fried cheese (usually haloumi or saganaki), stuffed vine leaves, yoghurt or aubergine dips, grilled octopus and so on.

And don't confuse these dishes with starters or nibbles. Meze can be served at any time of the day—even for breakfast—and with enough dishes on offer, can comprise an entire meal in their own right.

If this is the plan, groups of dishes will arrive at the table about four or five at a time, roughly grouped by type. For example, a selection of olives, tahini (a paste that is made by finely grinding sesame seeds), salad and yoghurt may be followed by dishes featuring vegetables and eggs, then small meat or fish dishes with their special accompaniments.

Given the abundance of food on offer, luckily, diners are not expected to clean every plate, but just to sample, share and enjoy whatever is on offer.

I like to think of meze as the ultimate grazing food, and best enjoyed with a few glasses of wine.

BAD TABOULI

For too long, the eating public have generally only had access to bad tabouli—sad little supermarket or salad bar specimens of wilted parsley and elderly mint. As a result, you'd be hard-pressed to find much flavour. It's also because most cooks tend to get the balance wrong—too much bulgur wheat, not enough herbs, and way too little lemon juice.

The dish should be a deep green, flecked with white from the wheat and the occasional red flash of tomato—not white, with red and green spots. The best way to achieve the right speckled effect is to add the bulgur last, as it's always far easier to add more than to take some out. And don't skimp on the lemon juice, the dish should have a distinctive zing, and some recipes add grated lemon zest to the dressing to ensure the dish has enough pizazz. Keep tasting as you combine the ingredients and add extra olive oil to give the flavours a boost.

QUINOA

Quinoa (pronounced 'keen-wah') is one of those grains that seem to bring out the self-righteousness in many cooks.

Yes, this age-old grain was eaten by people thousands of years ago (the ancient Incas called quinoa the 'mother grain') and yes, it's fat-free and gluten-free, and packed full of protein, fibre, iron and vitamins, and therefore good for you. But that doesn't mean it needs to be accompanied by a lecture.

Luckily, there is no need to feel intimidated, as the versatile little grain is delightfully easy to cook and, like rice and couscous and other pulses and grains, is great at sopping up and absorbing all kinds of flavours. In its simplest form, simply steam or boil the quinoa until just tender, then toss with a little olive oil and season well with salt and black pepper.

Quinoa comes in different varieties—the most common is white, but there is also red and black—and as it cooks, the outer germ around each grain twists outward, forming a little spiral 'tail' that is attached to the kernel. It is the light and fluffy softness of the grain and the relative crunch of the tail that give quinoa its interesting texture combination.

HERBED QUINOA

SERVES 4

Ingredients

1 tablespoon olive oil

185g quinoa

2 cups vegetable stock

4 garlic cloves, finely chopped

handful of fresh parsley, chopped

2 sprigs fresh thyme, stems removed, and leaves chopped

1 onion, finely chopped

salt and black pepper, to taste

2 teaspoons fresh lemon juice (optional)

Method

1. Heat the oil in a saucepan over medium heat. Add the quinoa and stir-fry until lightly browned (about 5 minutes).

2. Add the stock and bring to the boil.

3. Reduce to a simmer, cover, and cook for 15 minutes, or until the quinoa is just tender to the bite.

4. In a bowl, mix quinoa together with garlic, parsley, thyme and onion. Season to taste, sprinkle with lemon juice, and serve.

OTHER THINGS TO DO WITH QUINOA

* Substitute for plain steamed rice as an accompaniment for an array of sauce-based dishes—from curry to goulash. Cook following the method described opposite.
* Turn into a salad with roasted root vegetables, feta and balsamic dressing. Or opt for a Mediterranean twist with fresh basil leaves, roasted capsicums, finely sliced garlic and buffalo mozzarella. Try making a Middle Eastern-style salad, such as tabouli (see page 92), substituting the bulgur (cracked wheat) for quinoa.
* Turn into a pilaf by frying garlic, onion, chilli and spices, then cooking in chicken or vegetable stock and finally chucking in some spinach leaves until just wilted.
* Stuff a chicken or a capsicum using quinoa instead of breadcrumbs.
* Thicken a soup (in much the same way as you would use barley).
* If you are feeling adventurous, toss with a handful of chopped fruit and nuts, a splash of milk, and turn into a gluten-free porridge for breakfast.
* Cook and freeze with a curry for an instant meal when you're desperately hungry and can't be bothered cooking from scratch.

BAD QUINOA

First up, make sure that your quinoa hasn't gone off. This grain (more correctly, it's the seed of a plant) has a relatively high oil content so is best stored in a sealed container in the refrigerator to prevent it turning rancid.

Give it a rinse before you cook it—although most quinoa available in the supermarket has been pre-washed, you can lessen the chance of a bitter taste by giving it a good rinse. Make sure to use a very fine sieve, so that the little seeds don't disappear down the sink as you wash them.

And don't overcook it—you want it to be nutty and ever so slightly crunchy, rather than mushy. When it's ready, the germ will turn opaque and split from the seed so it resembles little curls. This generally takes about 15 minutes. Quinoa also holds a lot of water, so if you're cooking it in a lot of liquid (not like the absorption method above) you will need to drain it well after cooking or it's likely to turn your whole dish soggy. (Don't forget to use that fine sieve again.) You can help make it even lighter and fluffier—rather than wet and soggy—by letting it sit in a covered pot for 15 minutes after it has been cooked and drained.

FISH AND SHELLFISH

FISH EN PAPILLOTE 98
SALMON 100
FISH PIE 102
SQUID 104
MOULES MARINIÈRES 106
TEMPURA PRAWNS 108

CHAPTER 7

FISH AND SHELLFISH

Fish and shellfish offer the ultimate quickie for the hungry cook, often needing only a moment or two in a hot pan, over or under a grill, or in the oven.

Good seafood relies upon freshness though, so make sure that yours still smells of the sea (lake, river, or dam) and not of fish. A fishy smell is the good cook's clue that something is, well, fishy about your star ingredient.

FISH EN PAPILLOTE

The idea of cooking fish in a bag or parcel is so that you don't lose a single drop of flavour. The fish essentially steams in its own juices, and those of any liquids you might add, such as lemon juice. As an added benefit, it's a fat-free method of cooking—so long as you don't give into the strong temptation to add butter, that is.

Because the fish is covered from view, it's impossible to know when it is done by look or feel (you don't want to puncture the bag ahead of time), so it's important to stick rigidly to the timings given in the recipe below.

You can also use aluminium foil to seal your fish parcels, but be sure to oil them or else the fillets will stick and you'll end up with diners pulling shards of silver from between their teeth.

Traditionally, things cooked *en papillote* (in a parcel) form a complete meal, and should be served at the table so that each person gets the fun of opening the package and can smell the aromatic whoosh as the steam escapes.

SERVES 4

Ingredients

250g baby spinach leaves

3 spring onions, trimmed and thinly sliced

4 white fish fillets

½ bunch fresh coriander, washed and finely chopped

1 long red chilli, deseeded and finely chopped

handful of cherry or grape tomatoes, halved

salt and black pepper

1 tablespoon preserved lemon rind, finely chopped

2 tablespoons butter

juice of 1 lemon

1 egg white, lightly whisked, to seal the bags

Method

1. Preheat oven to 200°C (400°F).
2. Cut 4 large circles out of the baking paper, big enough to fit the fillets with ease. Grease lightly.
3. Divide the baby spinach between the 4 prepared circles, sprinkle with the spring onions and place a fish fillet on top. Strew each fillet with the coriander, chilli and tomatoes.
4. Season with salt and pepper, scatter the lemon rind over, put a knob of butter on the centre of each, then sprinkle with the juice.
5. Fold the piece of paper over to enclose the fish (you'll end up with a half-moon shape). Seal with egg white, or wrap again in aluminium foil to make a double bag.
6. Place the bagged up fillets onto a large baking sheet (or 2 small trays) and bake for 15 minutes.
7. To serve, simply pop a fish parcel on each plate, and allow diners to open their own packets at the table. Accompany with steamed rice or couscous to soak up the juices.

OTHER FLAVOUR COMBINATIONS

Fill your parcels with any number of tasty ingredients; just remember to take a moment to think about the ultimate flavour you want to create and choose items that will complement as opposed to overpower each other:

* Drunken herb-style: A splash of dry vermouth, thyme, parsley, dill, carrot, celery and finely sliced onion.
* Asian-style: Soy sauce, a dash of sherry, just a drop of sesame oil with a julienne (finely sliced batons) of ginger, garlic, snow or sugar snap peas, and coriander leaves. Or swap your white fish fillets for salmon and add sweet chilli sauce, spring onions, a few drops of fish sauce, a sprinkling of brown sugar and coriander leaves.
* Rainbow-style: White wine or dry vermouth, orange slices, fennel, red onion, chives or spring onions.
* Provençal-style: Chopped (and deseeded) tomatoes, olives, oregano, capers and garlic.

BAD FISH EN PAPILLOTE

The worst thing that can happen with 'fish in a bag' is that the bag isn't sealed completely and instead of opening it up to find a moist, aromatic piece of fish, the flesh is dry and flavourless. You can help prevent this happening by sealing the paper bag with a 'glue' of egg white.

One other thing to be wary of is the appearance of the final dish—yes, it's simple and yes, it's delicious, but because the fish is pale, you'll want some contrast on the plate so that it appeals to the eye as well as the tastebuds.

The recipe above uses tomatoes, chilli and spinach for a vibrant red-and-green contrast, but make sure that any side dishes also add to the overall appearance. Mashed potato, delicious as it is, probably won't cut it. Instead, think about serving some golden cubes of fried potato.

FISH AND SHELLFISH

SALMON

People have probably been eating griddled fish since the first caveman flicked a trout out of a river and onto a hot rock. But many today remain nervous about fish dishes, worrying that it will either be under or overcooked.

The simple method of griddling is a great way to get used to cooking fish, as it involves nothing more complicated than flicking your fillet into a searingly hot pan. The effect you're looking for is a crust on the outside and a centre that is moist, soft and just cooked.

A very cheffy thing to do is to leave the skin on, let it cook for a couple of minutes to get chargrill lines, then rotate it 90 degrees for a pretty cross-hatch pattern. The fish is cooked until it's nice and crispy then the cooking process is finished off in the oven. (You only need to worry about cross-hatching the skin side of the fillet, as the other side won't be seen).

To prepare the skin, wipe it down with kitchen towel and then, with a sharp knife, very finely score it (because when oiled skin hits a hot pan, it curls up).

During the cooking process, resist the temptation to poke and prod, or move the fillet around. Once done, you should also rest it for a few minutes, like you would a steak. A skewer inserted into the middle will enter easily when the fillet is done.

The griddling process works beautifully for other meaty fillets of fish—sea bass, snapper, swordfish and tuna, for example. Prawns and scallops come up a treat on the griddle too, but they won't need any time in the oven.

SERVES 4

Ingredients

4 x 200g thick salmon fillet portions, with the skin on

olive oil for drizzling

sea salt and black pepper

GRIDDLED SALMON

Method

1. Preheat oven to 180°C (350°F).

2. Tidy up the fillets by trimming any messy edges, and pat dry with kitchen towel.

3. Put a dry griddle pan over high heat until it's almost smoking. Drizzle the skin side of each fillet with a little olive oil and sprinkle with salt and pepper.

4. Turn the heat down to medium-high, and pop the fillets in the pan—laying it diagonally across the griddle bars. Leave for 90 seconds, then rotate to sear in the opposite direction.

5. Turn the fillets over and continue cooking for another 90 seconds, then slide them into the preheated oven for another 3 or 4 minutes or so.

SAUCING IT UP

Salmon cooked simply like this deserves a simply delicious sauce—hollandaise (see page 132) immediately springs to mind.

Or how about a tangy lime butter sauce, made simply by puréeing together a fat clove of garlic, ½ cup of lime juice, and some salt and freshly ground black pepper. With the motor running, add ½ cup of melted butter and blend until emulsified, for about 30 seconds.

Another easy option is a vinaigrette (see page 134) or—even simpler yet—a squeeze of fresh lemon juice and sprinkling of roughly chopped fresh coriander leaves.

You can also alter the flavour of the salmon itself by using a herbed or spiced olive oil at the very beginning—lemon-pressed olive oil, for example, or perhaps an oil that is steeped in garlic and herbs.

Side dishes can be as light or as filling as you wish—salad for a warm summer's day or more substantial roast potatoes (see page 64).

BAD SALMON

Overcook fillets of fish at your peril. This will make the flesh dry and tasteless, rather than juicy. So while salmon has lots of oil and is more forgiving than other types of fish, it's best cooked hot and fast.

You'll know it's done when the flesh changes from translucent to opaque, and a glaze forms on the outside. Inside, it should be moist and flaky. (Don't forget that it will keep cooking once you remove it from the heat source.)

The other cardinal rule is not to drown it in sauce or over-flavour the flesh with too many strong ingredients—you want the flavour of the fish to shine through.

FISH PIE

Fish pie makes for the perfect Saturday night dinner—ideally after a morning spent at the market collecting all sorts of fresh ocean goodies. It's the variety of fish that makes a good pie, so bulk it up with firm white fillets, then add colour and flavour with some fresh pink salmon fillets, some undyed smoked fish (perhaps haddock), and a handful of plump little prawns. All this gets combined with a creamy, savoury sauce, then hidden underneath a crowd-pleasing crust of fluffy mash. Some recipes moisten the filling with crème fraîche, but for a perfect fish pie you really need to make a sauce from scratch.

Essentially, it's a béchamel sauce (see page 130), but here the seafood is first poached in the milk, which gives the final sauce a far richer, deeper flavour. Use full-cream milk for the creamiest texture. If you want to bulk out the filling, or turn it into an all-in-one meal, add some cooked carrot and peas or spinach, which has the added bonus of not requiring any pre-cooking. Leeks can be swapped for the onions—neither are strictly necessary, but add greatly to the taste. Hard-boiled eggs are another traditional addition, but don't add them if you're planning to freeze the dish at any stage.

SERVES 6-8

Ingredients

1.25kg skinless fish fillets (a mix of white and pink, for example cod and salmon), no bones!

250g smoked fish

600ml full-cream milk

handful of fresh parsley (stalks and leaves), washed and roughly chopped

6 peppercorns

1 bay leaf

60g butter

60g flour

splash of dry white wine or sherry

2 medium onions, chopped and sautéed until golden

2 tablespoons capers

Method

1. Preheat the oven to 180°C (350°F).

2. Place the seafood in a saucepan with the milk. Add the parsley, peppercorns and bay leaf, and warm until almost boiling. Simmer for 5 minutes, until the fish is tender and opaque. Remove from the heat, cover and leave to steep for about half an hour.

3. Boil potatoes until tender, drain, and mash with butter until soft (adding a little milk if it is too thick). Season.

4. Strain the fish and milk mixture, reserving the milk. Discard the parsley, bay leaf and peppercorns. Break the fish into large chunks and place these in a large ovenproof dish.

5. Melt the butter in a saucepan over medium heat and then add the flour. Cook for 1-2 minutes, stirring constantly, until a light golden colour, then gradually add the wine and milk, whisking until smooth. Stir over moderate heat for about 5 minutes until thickened.

FISH PIE

zest of 1 large lemon

extra fresh parsley or dill, finely chopped, optional

For the topping

1.8kg potatoes
(or sweet potatoes, or a mix of spuds and parsnips or celeriac, peeled and cut into chunks)

60g butter

milk, for thinning, if necessary

salt and black pepper

parmesan or pecorino, freshly grated

6. Remove the sauce from the heat and tip in the cooked onions, capers and lemon zest. Chop and add a few extra parsley or dill leaves if you wish. Taste for seasoning.

7. Tip sauce over the fish and tumble so that the fish is lightly coated. Spoon or pipe the prepared mash over the fish. Bake for 40 minutes in the preheated oven until crisp and golden, and the filling is bubbling.

8. Leave for 5 minutes before serving. With peas, of course.

Note—the dish can also be assembled ahead of time and refrigerated, but bring it back to room temperature before cooking, otherwise you risk burning the top while the innards are still cold.

POSH PIE

To dress up your pie for a more formal occasion, you can use a piping bag to pipe the potato in a pretty pattern. For this, the mash needs to be smooth as possible, so you may need to thin it down with a little extra milk.

Another favourite from the 19th century was something enticingly called Fish and Potato Mould—you'll need about half as much mash again for this. To assemble, butter a pudding basin or decorative mould and line it with some of the mash—you'll probably use about two-thirds of it, depending on the size of your mould. It needs to be about 1.5cm thick, so the walls don't collapse as you turn it out.

Fill with the prepared fish mixture, top with the remaining mash and bake as before. Turn out of the mould carefully, so as not to break the shape, and serve immediately.

BAD FISH PIE

This comfort food favourite has been mucked about in so many ways that it's hard to know where to start. One memorable version I was served involved tuna (tinned), sweet chilli sauce, peas and mash—all topped off with crushed cornflakes. Somewhat less horrifying versions ignore the mash altogether and go for either a pastry top (puff or shortcrust). Only genuine clouds of fluffy mash will soak up the sauce.

Bad fish is another no-no. Go for freshness and variety, of course, but expensive scallops are wasted here and mussels tend to get chewy.

FISH AND SHELLFISH

SQUID

Squid is one of those funny creatures that's either great cooked fast and furious over a high temperature, or low and slow. Should you fall between these two extremes, you're likely to experience the unpleasant sensation that you're chewing on rubber.

Being a contrary kind of beast, it's no surprise to discover that while squid is a cousin of both the octopus and the cuttlefish, it is actually a kind of mollusc with an internal shell. Calamari is just one of many types of squid, and is generally more tender and hence more expensive at your fishmonger.

This recipe involves long, slow braising in liquid, but you can also bake squid in the oven, stuffed with breadcrumbs and herbs, and covered in a rich tomato sauce. Or if you're short of time, think about flash barbecuing or pan-frying it, or perhaps deep-frying in a salt and pepper batter (see page 108 for tempura).

Of course, different cultures have their own particular favourites—Greeks love it braised for hours with fennel and tomato, the Spanish eat it stuffed and cooked in its own ink (*chipirones en su tinta*) and Koreans like it in a spicy stir-fry (*ojingeo bokkeum*). Croats cook it with rice and squid ink to produce *crna riz*—essentially a black risotto, while in Italy it turns up in salads, soups and pasta sauces, and the Chinese, of course, can't resist it in a dumpling.

SQUID, CHORIZO AND CANNELLINI CASSEROLE

SERVES 6-8

Ingredients

- 3-4 tablespoons olive oil
- 1 onion, peeled and sliced
- 5 large garlic cloves, thinly sliced
- 225g chorizo sausage, peeled and cut into 1cm slices
- 1 stalk of celery, finely chopped
- 2 carrots, peeled and sliced
- 1 teaspoon dried chilli flakes
- 1 teaspoon smoked sweet paprika
- 1kg squid tubes and tentacles, cleaned and cut into chunks
- 1½ cans (600g) cannellini beans, drained

Method

1. Heat the olive oil over medium heat, and add the onion and garlic—fry until golden.
2. Add the chorizo chunks, stir and cook for a couple of minutes until the sausage begins to leak its oil and colour. Then add the celery, carrot, chilli flakes, smoked paprika and squid.
3. Sauté for 4-5 minutes until the veggies soften. Add the beans and stir.
4. Tip in the wine, chopped tomatoes, lemon zest and bay leaf.
5. Bring to a slow simmer, then lower the heat and cover for around 40 minutes. Take a peek every so often to make sure it isn't drying out. Give it a stir.

SQUID

350ml red wine

400g can chopped tomatoes

grated zest of 1 lemon

1 bay leaf

sea salt and black pepper

handful of fresh flat-leaf parsley, finely chopped

crusty bread and lemon wedges, to serve

6. After 40 minutes, uncover and turn the heat up slightly to reduce the liquid. Simmer for another 30 minutes. The sauce will continue to thicken up with the starch from the beans.

7. Season to taste before serving in bowls scattered with fresh parsley, and with wedges of lemon and crusty bread for people to help themselves.

HOW TO CLEAN SQUID

Holding the body firmly, grasp the head and pull gently, twisting if necessary, to pull the head away from the body without breaking the ink sac. The internal body and tentacles will come with it. Cut the tentacles from the head just below the eyes. Trim any long ones level with the rest. At the centre of the tentacles is a small hard beak. Squeeze to remove and discard.

Set aside the tentacles to use (they're edible and tasty). If the recipe calls for ink, reserve it; otherwise discard the head and ink sac.

At the top of the body, there is a clear piece of cartilage (the squid's internal shell), kind of like a plastic shoehorn. Pull it out and discard. If the squid has a spotty skin, pull it off and discard. Cut the squid open, and scrape any more innards out and discard.

Under cold running water, wash the tube carefully, inside and out, to get rid of any sand or remnants of guts, and wash the tentacles. Cut into slices, or score the squid and cut into pieces.

BAD SQUID

It's all about striking a happy medium—two minutes over high heat is plenty, beyond that, you need to cook squid for at least 30 minutes to an hour to tenderise it.

There is also lots of handed-down lore about how to make doubly sure your squid turns out tender—soaking it in milk overnight, soaking in lemon juice for five minutes just before you cook it, or pounding it with a meat mallet.

Of course, should you not feel confident in cleaning and preparing the squid yourself, simply ask your trusty fishmonger to do it for you. Squid also freezes well so don't be afraid of the frozen variety. Just defrost it in the fridge, and if not using straight away, store in an airtight container for up to three days.

MOULES MARINIÈRES

Otherwise known as Sailor's Mussels, *moules marinières* is a simple classic dish that's popular in France, Belgium and the Netherlands, and often comes with a side of *frites*, or fries.

Essentially, it's just mussels lightly steamed in wine or beer or cider, with some flavourings such as garlic or parsley added. The creamy broth is delicious, and demands lots of crusty bread for sopping it up. However, there are a few tricks to getting it right, including:

1. *Clean your mussels properly*
Mussels must be thoroughly cleaned and rinsed several times before cooking—unless, of course, you buy them ready prepared. Wild mussels need to be scrubbed with a stiff brush to remove any barnacles, sand or grit, and the beard (the tough, stringy growth that keeps the mussel connected to the colony while in the water) must also be removed. This can be done by pinching the beard between thumb and forefinger, giving it a sharp tug and pulling it away or cutting it off with a sharp knife. Rinse wild mussels several times but do not allow them to rest in it, as fresh water will kill them.

2. *Use your widest saucepan, ideally one with a glass lid*
This allows the cooking liquid and steam to reach the mussels easily. Since the mussels will probably be in more than one layer, jiggle the pot every so often so they all get a good go in every position. A glass lid allows you to see when the mussels are open, so you can dive in and retrieve them.

3. *Don't use too much liquid*
Mussels should not be covered with liquid and boiled like a spud. They need to steam, not boil. They'll also add some of their own juices as they cook, but this can be quite salty so be careful with extra seasoning.

4. *Stop cooking the mussels as soon as their shells open*
Remove mussels from the heat as soon as their shells open. Since they usually open at different times, depending on how keen they are to cling onto life, use a slotted spoon or tongs to carefully remove the open mussels while the rest continue cooking. (If you don't have a glass-lidded pot, take a peek after three minutes and remove any open ones, then leave the top off while the others finish steaming, taking them out as they open.)

5. *Toss any mussels that don't open*
If any mussels don't open, they'd probably turned up their toes (fins? shells?) before landing in your pot. Toss them out and enjoy all the others.

MOULES MARINIÈRES

SERVES 4

Ingredients

¾ cup dry white wine

1 tablespoon butter

1 large onion, very finely chopped

4 garlic cloves, crushed

2kg black mussels, scrubbed, debearded

2 tablespoons thickened cream

½ cup fresh flat-leaf parsley, chopped

fries and/or crusty bread, to serve

Method

1. Boil the wine in a small saucepan for 30 seconds then set aside. This removes the harsh tang of the alcohol and leaves just the flavour.

2. Melt the butter in a large saucepan over high heat, then add the onion and garlic and stir for 10 seconds. Add the wine and bring to a boil.

3. Add the mussels, cover with a lid and cook for 2-3 minutes or until they open. Discard any that don't open.

4. Add the cream and parsley and stir well. Season to taste, although you may not need anything as the mussels will release a little salt water when they open, which can be enough to season the dish perfectly.

5. Serve the mussels in a large, warmed serving bowl or ladle out into individual soup plates. Remember finger bowls and good-quality bread to mop up the juices.

COOKING WITH GAS

Try adding Madras curry powder with the onion and garlic, omit the cream, and finish the dish with lemon juice and fresh coriander.

Or for a Thai version, add chilli, garlic, lemongrass and a Kaffir lime leaf with the onion and garlic, and replace the cream with a dash of coconut milk. You can even replace the wine with cider for a taste of Normandy.

BAD MOULES MARINIERES

Lazy cooks don't wash their mussels properly, and they certainly don't care about timing. That explains why, even in some restaurants, you may dive into a bowl of mussels only to end up with a mouthful of grit and something resembling a snail that's been decimated. Mussels should be soft and yielding, not hard and chewy.

If in doubt, buy your mussels already cleaned and de-bearded. If doing it yourself, do not scrub the shells too hard as the colour will transfer during cooking giving an unappetising grey colour to the finished dish.

TEMPURA PRAWNS

What's not to love about golden prawns in a crispy batter, scattered with fiery chillies, onion, salt and pepper? A staple on many Asian restaurant menus, these prawns are also surprisingly easy to cook at home, and are great to serve as nibbles with drinks or as part of a large feast.

The only real trick is in the batter, which needs to be whisked together very quickly so that you don't lose the air bubbles. Don't worry if there are lumps in it—these disappear when the batter is cooked.

This tempura batter is also brilliant with thin strips of fish, squid, scallops or veggies, such as snow peas and eggplant.

Here the prawns are served topped with a deep-fried garnish of garlic, spring onion and chilli, but you can also serve plain with a dipping sauce of sweet chilli or Asian Kewpie mayonnaise (made with egg yolks instead of whole eggs and rice vinegar), perhaps with some finely diced spring onions stirred through.

SERVES 4

Ingredients

1 teaspoon each of black, white and Sichuan peppercorns

1 teaspoon sea salt

85g flour

16 large raw prawns, peeled

vegetable oil, for deep-frying

Method

1. Crush the peppercorns and the salt in a mortar until finely ground. Mix with the flour and spread out on a large plate. Toss the prawns in the seasoned flour then shake off any excess.

2. To make the tempura batter, mix the flour, cornflour and bicarbonate of soda together, then add the water, ice and egg white. Whisk gently to just bring the mixture together into a batter, but don't overdo it.

3. Heat the oil in a wok or deep-fryer to about 170°C (325°F). If you don't have a thermometer, give one of the prawns a test run—simply dip in batter and toss in the hot oil; if the oil is hot enough, your prawn should cook in about 2-3 minutes. The batter will be light, crispy and golden.

4. When the oil is hot enough, toss about a third of the prawns into the bowl of batter and stir them gently around to coat. Drop into the hot oil and fry until ready.

5. Lift out with a slotted spoon and allow to drain on kitchen paper while you prepare the next 2 batches of prawns.

TEMPURA PRAWNS

For the tempura batter

50g flour

50g cornflour

¼ teaspoon bicarbonate of soda

150ml ice-cold sparkling water

2 ice cubes

1 large egg white, whisked to a froth

To serve

4 garlic cloves, sliced

1 red chilli, sliced

4 spring onions, sliced

6. Deep-fry the garlic, chilli and spring onions for about 30 seconds. Or you can leave out this step, and serve them raw.

7. Serve the prawns immediately, sprinkled with the garlic, chilli and onion.

GOING THE RAW PRAWN

The easiest way to peel, clean and prepare a raw prawn ready for cooking is to:

⋆ Rip off its head with a twisting motion.

⋆ Hold the prawn by the tail, and with your thumb, work your way under the shell, lifting the shell up and away from the body.

⋆ Remove the black vein (its digestive tract) that runs the length of its back.

⋆ If you want to butterfly your prawn, as for a barbecue, simply pop the shelled prawn on a chopping board, and use a very sharp knife to slit it in half lengthwise from the head to its tail until it's almost, but not quite, cut through. Flatten it out into a kind of prawn version of a butterfly shape.

BAD TEMPURA PRAWNS

Claggy batter makes for a claggy mouthful, so make sure that you don't over-whisk the mixture—this knocks the air out of it, and you'll end up with something resembling wallpaper paste, rather than a light-as-a-feather batter.

You should also be careful not to overcrowd the frying pan as this lowers the temperature of the oil, and you'll end up with soggy specimens instead of the crisp little critters you're aiming for. Instead, fry the prawns in batches.

MEATS

STEAK 112
ROAST CHICKEN 114
BEEF CASSEROLE 116
HAMBURGER 118
SAUSAGES 120
PORK STIR-FRY 122
ROAST PORK 124
ROAST LAMB 126

CHAPTER 8

MEATS

From the nose to the tail of the animal, from game and other red meat to poultry, no other food group offers such variety as meat. Preparing it well is seen as the mark of a good and confident cook, but different cuts from the one animal can also be deceptively versatile.

Think of how a simple chook can be roasted whole (see page 114), filleted and turned into nuggets (see page 44) or slivered and stir-fried. Likewise, a tender beef fillet can be grilled as a steak (see page 112) or minced and turned into a burger (see page 118), while chewier cuts such as stewing steak are full of connective tissue and made for cooking long and slow in the oven until they dissolve into a gelatinous gloop— the perfect recipe for an inattentive or beginner cook.

STEAK

On the face of it, nothing could be easier than cooking a steak, right? You put it in a pan, cook it, and take it out. The truth is, though, that even BBQ diehards and chefs don't always get it right. But follow the guidelines below, and you'll get perfect steak, every time:

★ Allow the meat to come to room temperature first. That means taking it out of the fridge at least an hour before cooking.
★ Make sure the barbecue, frying pan or griddle is both clean and roaring hot before you add your steak. If you flick a few drops of water onto it, they should sizzle and evaporate immediately.
★ Oil the steak, not the pan. You don't want the steak to be stewing in moisture, as this will toughen the meat and stop it searing properly.
★ Just before you cook the steak, season with salt and pepper, as this will help form the crust. Don't do this too early though, as salt will draw moisture from the flesh, making it drier and tougher.
★ Once the steak hits the pan, leave it alone. If you fiddle around with it, it won't develop a nice crust.
★ Always use tongs to flip the steak over—sticking a fork in it will allow moisture to escape and it will end up dry and leathery.
★ Once done to your satisfaction, allow the meat to rest before being served. This allows the muscle fibres to relax after having tensed up in horror in the hot pan. A steak that's been rested is far more tender than one that's been served immediately. Simply pop it on a plate, cover loosely with foil and leave for 5 minutes before serving.
★ Serve as is, or with a sauce of your choosing. Alternatively, you can take a leaf out of a certain celebrity chef's book and throw it on a wooden board that's been covered in a slick of olive oil and chopped fresh herbs. Slice the steak on an angle, mop the pieces in the herby oil and serve.

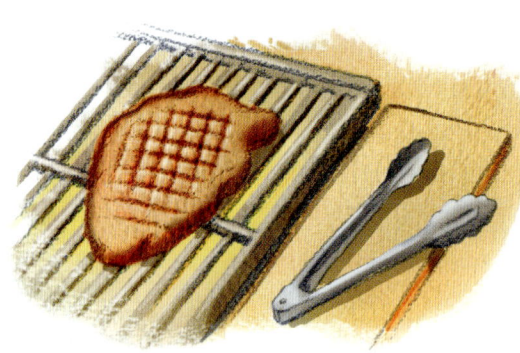

LEMON PEPPER STEAK

SERVES 8

Ingredients

⅓ cup Dijon mustard

2 tablespoons lemon juice, plus 1 tablespoon finely grated lemon rind

2 tablespoons black pepper

⅓ cup finely chopped fresh flat-leaf parsley leaves

8 x 150g steaks (scotch fillet for preference and tenderness)

olive oil cooking spray

Method

1. Combine the mustard and lemon juice in a bowl. Combine the cracked pepper, parsley and lemon rind on a plate.
2. Using a pastry brush, brush one side of a steak with the mustard mixture, then press that same side into the pepper mixture. Repeat with the remaining steaks.
3. Preheat a barbecue, heavy-based frying pan or griddle on medium-high.
4. Spray the steaks with oil and cook for 2 minutes, seasoning side down. Turn the steaks and cook for a further 2 minutes, or until cooked to your liking.
5. Transfer the cooked steaks to a platter and cover loosely with foil. Set aside for 5 minutes to rest then serve with spuds or crusty bread and salads.

DONE TO PERFECTION

To know whether a steak is done or not give it a prod with a finger and feel how the meat reacts:

* Very soft = rare (roughly 2 minutes each side)
* Springy = medium (3 minutes each side)
* Very firm = well done (4 minutes each side)

If you want to practice without burning through a week's grocery money, pinch your thumb and index finger together on one hand. With your other index finger, touch the fleshy part of your palm at the base of your thumb. That's what rare steak feels like. Pinch your middle finger and thumb, and you've got medium. When you pinch your ring finger and thumb, the springiness of the fleshy bit equals medium to well done, and your pinky and thumb well done. Easy.

BAD STEAK

Most problems arise during cooking (see above), but you should also be careful about the cut you choose—the more the muscle moved while the animal was alive, the tougher it will be.

For tenderness, you can't go past eye fillet. Next up is scotch fillet and sirloin, which snuggle near the spine. Rump from the inside of the leg has seen a bit of action, and will be a bit tougher, but can be tastier, too. Rib-eye and T-bone are two on-the-bone options, and are generally juicier as the bone protects the meat from drying out. That said, even the best cut of meat can be ruined with age. Look for a deep red colour and white fat, rather than yellow.

ROAST CHICKEN

At its simplest, roast chicken is nothing more than a bird that's been killed, plucked, gutted and shoved into an oven, where the heat works its miracles. The next step along the path of culinary evolution is to shove a lemon up its bum, along with a few sprigs of fresh thyme, rosemary, sage or tarragon. Then drizzle with olive oil, sprinkle with plenty of freshly ground black pepper and a little salt, and you're ready.

For a full-on traditional roast chicken dinner, though, the secret is in the timing, getting everything ready at the same time, so that the chicken is golden and perfectly cooked, the potatoes soft inside and crispy on the outside (see page 64), and the greens done just right. And the gravy too—don't forget the gravy.

For perfectly crispy skin, first tip boiling water all over your bird, then pat thoroughly dry with kitchen towel, and leave uncovered in the fridge overnight. This helps dry out the skin.

For more succulent flesh, take the bird out of the fridge about an hour before cooking.

Stuff the chicken just before you roast it. If you stuff it too early, the bacteria from the raw chicken juice may contaminate the stuffing.

SERVES 4-6

Ingredients

1 large, free-range chicken, about 1.5kg

sea salt and black pepper

butter, for smearing over the bird

For the stuffing

25g butter

1 tablespoon olive oil

1 large onion, finely chopped

3 cups fresh white breadcrumbs

½ cup chopped fresh mixed herbs (such as thyme, sage, parsley and tarragon) or 2 teaspoons dried mixed herbs, if you must

zest and juice of 1 lemon

1 egg, beaten

salt and black pepper

FRESH HERB STUFFED CHICKEN

Method

1. Preheat the oven to 190°C (375°F).

2. To make the stuffing, gently heat the butter and oil in a large frying pan over low heat and cook the onion for 10 minutes until soft and translucent.

3. Remove from the heat and tip into a bowl. Stir in the breadcrumbs, herbs, lemon zest, beaten egg and salt and pepper, and mix well to bind the mixture together. Use some lemon juice to moisten it if it still looks and feels crumbly. Allow the stuffing to cool completely.

4. If they're present, remove the giblets and neck from the chicken (save these to make stock, if you wish).

5. Season the inside of the bird with salt and pepper and an extra squeeze of lemon juice, then fill the cavity with the stuffing, pushing it well up inside. Any leftover can be baked alongside the bird in a greased ovenproof dish (but don't place in the oven until the last 20 minutes of cooking time).

6. Place the chicken on one side in a roasting tin, and roast for 25 minutes. Flip it over to its other side, baste with the pan juices and roast for another 25 minutes. Turning and basting helps distribute the heat evenly, and keeps the flesh moist.

7. Remove the roasting tin from the oven again, and gently turn the chicken over so its breast is facing up. Baste and cook for another 20 minutes. If you have extra stuffing to cook, add it now.

8. To test if the chicken is ready, insert a skewer into the thickest part of the thigh—the juices should run clear. When ready, put it on a platter, cover it loosely with foil and allow it to sit for 10-15 minutes. This 'resting' period allows the flesh to relax and makes the bird easier to carve and more succulent.

GREAT GRAVY

This is best flung together while your chicken is resting—pop the roasting tin over a low flame, then stir in a tablespoon of flour and let it sizzle until it turns into a golden brown, sandy paste. Gradually pour in a cup of liquid (stock, wine, boiling water or a mix of any of these), stirring constantly to avoid lumps forming.

Once the sauce has thickened, allow to simmer for a couple of minutes more, using a wooden spoon to scrape any lovely sticky bits from the bottom. Strain into a small saucepan, season to taste and leave on very low heat. Add any juices that ooze from the bird while it is resting or when you carve it.

BAD ROAST CHICKEN

Undercook a roast chook at your peril, as there's nothing worse than ripping into a bird that's golden on the outside only to find that it's still running with blood on the inside. Overcooking is almost as bad, turning even a well-bred bird into something dry and stringy. Using a meat thermometer will help you get it right every time. All you have to do is shove this simple bit of kitchen kit into the thickest part of the thigh, making sure not to touch any bone.

At somewhere between 65-70°C (150-160°F), the bird will be ready. Remember that you need to rest your chook for about 15 minutes and the bird will continue cooking after you remove it from the oven. If you don't have a thermometer to hand, insert a skewer or knife into the thickest part of the thigh and the juices should run clear. If they look pink, return the chicken to the oven and cook a little longer. As a rough guide, a 1.5kg chicken will be perfectly roasted after 80 minutes at 190°C (375°F). It doesn't matter what you've rubbed onto it, stuffed into it, or scattered around it—this timing practically never changes.

BEEF CASSEROLE

There's lots of science involved in cooking a good casserole, but the only thing a home cook really needs to know is:

* You need to sear the meat first, before immersing it in liquid and cooking slowly for a long time. This helps bring out the flavour—the whole point of eating really.
* The liquid surrounding the meat should never boil—you just want it to bubble and plop, rather than spitting furiously. You can either cook it on the hob if you're brave (and attentive) or pop it in the oven at no more than 150°C (300°F).
* Even though this isn't generally a fatty dish, surprising amounts of fat will come out of the meat. Skim this from the surface of the casserole—use a metal spoon while it's cooking. Alternatively, cook the whole thing, chill it, and then scoop off the congealed fat.
* If you overcook it, the meat will appear dry and stringy, as all of the juices will have leached into the sauce. In this case, feed the meat to the dog, and save the sauce to coat some glorious fresh, homemade pasta (see page 76).

MAKES 6

Ingredients

⅓ cup plain flour

salt and black pepper

750g chuck steak (stewing steak), excess fat trimmed, cut into 3cm pieces

1 tablespoon olive oil

200g bacon or pancetta, diced or sliced into matchsticks

2 tablespoons butter

2 onions, peeled and chopped

Method

1. Place the flour in a large clean plastic bag and season well with salt and pepper. Add the beef, hold the top of the bag tightly shut and gently toss about until the cubes are evenly coated. Shake off any excess flour.

2. Heat half the oil in a large flameproof casserole dish over medium to high heat. Add the bacon and cook until golden, then remove with a slotted spoon and reserve.

3. Add the rest of the olive oil and enough beef to easily fit without overcrowding. Cook for 3-4 minutes or until browned all over. Transfer to a heatproof bowl.

BEEF CASSEROLE

3 garlic cloves, peeled and chopped

4 carrots, peeled and cut into 2cm thick slices

95g tomato paste

250ml red wine

500ml good-quality beef stock

1 x 400g can diced tomatoes

3 bay leaves

6 sprigs fresh thyme

500g small button mushrooms, sautéed until tender

fresh parsley, chopped, to serve

4. Cook the rest of the beef in batches, making sure the pan gets hot enough again between each batch.

5. Add the onion, garlic and carrot to the casserole dish and cook, stirring occasionally, for 5 minutes or until the vegetables are tender. Add the tomato paste and stir to combine, giving it a couple of minutes to cook with the other veggies.

6. Finally, return the beef cubes and bacon to the pan. Add the wine, stock, diced tomatoes, bay leaves and thyme, and stir to combine. Cover and simmer over low heat, stirring occasionally, for 2 hours.

7. Add the sautéed mushrooms and continue cooking for another 20 minutes. By now, the meat should be meltingly tender when prodded with a fork.

8. Season with more salt and pepper, divide among warm serving plates and sprinkle with parsley. This is great with some fluffy mash (see page 65) and lightly cooked greens. Or a baked spud and salad.

RINGING THE CHANGES

While this recipe is for a classic French-style casserole, you can also turn it into an Anglo-Irish version by replacing the wine with Guinness, and adding dumplings. The easiest of these are made from a basic savoury scone dough (see page 163), which is simply shaped into balls and dropped on top of the casserole for the last 15-20 minutes of cooking, until risen and golden brown.

Or stick to the dish's origins and turn it Provençal with the addition of some strips of fresh orange peel and lavender sprigs. This recipe also makes the perfect filling for a pie (see shortcrust pastry recipe on page 148) or the leftovers can be topped with mash for a flash cottage pie.

BAD BEEF CASSEROLE

Stringy, tough, lack of gravy—all these elements suggest that the dish has been either over or undercooked. Stewing steak is called this for a good reason—because it comes from heavily used muscles, it's not marbled with fat or especially flavoursome. Instead, it's full of lots of connective tissue that must be slowly and gently dissolved into gelatin before the meat becomes tender. Like most slow-cooked dishes, it's even better when gently reheated and eaten the next day.

HAMBURGER

The humble hamburger is not so humble these days, thanks to the current trend for high-end restaurants and 'celebrity' chefs to reinvent it with ingredients such as Wagyu beef, beetroot 'caviar', *foie gras* and brioche buns. But before you start experimenting, first you need to master the basics of a burger that's juicy, perfectly seasoned, charred on the outside and an even rosy pink throughout the inside.

The right mince is essential—choose prime grade meat (beef traditionally, although lamb and pork work well, too) and ask your butcher to mince it for you on the spot, rather than buying it prepackaged. The ready-prepared stuff is often made from trimmings left over from steaks, roasts and stewing meat, and once it has been squished down, it's impossible to regain a light texture. The mince should not be too finely ground, as your patties will be harder to work with and more likely to crumble, and any additional ingredients—such as onion or garlic—need to be carefully chopped or minced, or the patty will fall apart around them. You should also steer clear of meat that is too lean, as the perfect burger requires a good dose of fat—around 15-20 per cent. Remember, lots of the fat will drain off as you cook, so starting out too lean will make for a dry burger. When shaping your patty, roll the mince into a ball and press it flat to get a good, round shape. Chilling it ahead of cooking will help your patties hold their shape.

As for cooking, there's really only one way to cook a burger—flat out, on a really hot surface. When the raw meat hits this, it will sizzle immediately and stick. Don't panic—as the bottom of the patty cooks, fat will ooze out and the burger will let go. This is your cue to flip it. The bottom should be nicely charred. When the second side is done, flip them again and turn down the heat. Continue cooking for another few minutes, until done, and let sit for a minute or two before you serve.

Finally, filling. Use really ripe tomatoes; a watery tomato doesn't add any taste. Burgers work brilliantly with relishes, mustards and pickles, which add a piquant tang.

SERVES 4

Ingredients

750g beef mince

1 onion, finely chopped

2 garlic cloves, crushed

1 tablespoon Worcestershire sauce

1 tablespoon tomato sauce

Method

1. Place the beef, onion, garlic, sauces, parsley, chilli flakes, breadcrumbs and egg in a bowl. Season with salt and pepper and use your hands to combine the mixture. Form into 4 thick-ish patties and refrigerate for at least 20 minutes.

1 tablespoon chopped fresh parsley

sprinkle of dried chilli flakes

1 cup fresh breadcrumbs

1 free-range egg

salt and black pepper

olive oil cooking spray

4 slices cheese—Cheddar or Swiss, or something that melts easily

4 hamburger buns

To serve

Your choice of rocket, baby cos lettuce, baby spinach, roasted red capsicums, very ripe tomatoes, crispy bacon rashers, avocado, tomato sauce, mustard, pickles, onion jam, fried onions, mayonnaise—the list is pretty much endless

2. Wash and dry the salad leaves, leaving not a speck of moisture. Prepare any other condiments and pop them, ready to roll, in separate serving dishes. Preheat the oven to 120°C (250°F).

3. Heat a griddle pan or barbecue to high. Lightly spray the patties with oil and cook for 2–3 minutes, each side, until cooked through. Place a cheese slice on each patty for last the minute of cooking.

4. Meanwhile, toast the buns or warm through in the oven. Place a patty on each bun and allow diners to top them up with their choice of extra fillings and condiments.

ONLY IN AMERICA...

Would you find a burger bar called the Heart Attack Grill, specialising in such delights as the 'Quadruple Bypass Burger', which comes with a 910g beef patty and 20 slices of bacon, and packs a whopping 8000 calories. The only available side dish is Flatliner Fries—skinny chips deep-fried in pure lard.

To give you an idea of the physical impact of eating all this, anyone managing to finish the QBB is ceremoniously taken back to their car in a wheelchair at the end of the meal by a waitress dressed in a nurse's uniform.

BAD HAMBURGER

With hamburgers, as with most things in life, you can have too much of a good thing. Massive patties that require you to dislocate your jaw to get a mouthful are a case in point. So too are burgers piled so high that they are nigh on impossible to lift off the plate without starting an avalanche of fillings. As a rule of thumb, anything that can't be held in two hands is too big.

SAUSAGES

Pork, beef, lamb or a mixture. Fresh, dried, cured, aged or smoked. Pretty much every cuisine in the world has experimented at some time with shoving ground-up meat into a casing, be it animal or artificial.

There's bright red tangy chorizo from Spain, 'bangers' from England, spicy Turkish *sucuk*, *merguez* from North Africa, Greek *loukanika* and the dried Chinese *lap cheong* (normally smoked, sweetened and seasoned with rosewater, rice wine and soy sauce).

To cook most sausages perfectly, you need to bring them up to room temperature first. Some cooks swear by poaching them first before frying or grilling (essential in the case of *lap cheong*); others just pop them straight into a hot pan.

And beware of any old-fashioned advice from your grandmother that sausages must be pricked or they risk exploding. This may have been the case back in the days of rationing after the war, when sausages were pumped full of water to bulk them out, but these days even the poorest specimen is unlikely to split and spit.

Whether grilling or frying (frying is my preference) just be sure to cook them slowly, otherwise they may end up burnt on the outside and raw on the inside. You can also just throw them in a roasting pan with a slosh of olive oil, some quartered red onions, cherry tomatoes, and some wine or cider, and cook in the oven for 45 minutes or until the sausages are browned, the onions soft and the tomatoes slightly charred. Scrumptious served on top of some red radicchio leaves, with crusty bread.

Sausage sandwiches aside, the following recipe is great for an easy one-pot supper, brings a delicious warmth to a cold winter's evening and is also an excellent way of using up any leftover sausages.

SPICY ITALIAN SAUSAGE AND LENTIL STEW

SERVES 4

Ingredients

8 good-quality pork sausages—look for ones with lots of herbs and a garlic flavour

olive oil, for frying

2 onions, chopped

2 garlic cloves, crushed

pinch of chilli flakes

3 carrots, cut into small dice

Method

1. Cook the whole sausages in a little olive oil in a large pan until golden brown all over.

2. Take the sausages out of the pan, keep them to one side, then add the chopped onions and garlic to the pan and cook until softened.

3. Add the chilli flakes, carrots and celery to the onion mix, and cook for another 5 minutes.

SAUSAGES

3 sticks celery, cut into small dice

4 sprigs fresh rosemary, needles stripped and very finely chopped

1 teaspoon fennel seeds

2 cans (800g) chopped tomatoes

400ml white wine or chicken stock

6 tablespoons green lentils

4. Add most of the rosemary (saving a little to sprinkle over the finished dish), the fennel seeds, tomatoes, wine or stock and lentils.

5. Slice each sausage diagonally into thick chunks then tip back into the pan. Simmer with the lid just a little ajar for about 30 minutes, or until the lentils are tender and the sauce is rich and thick.

BANGERS AND FACTS

★ Sausages were mentioned in Homer's *Odyssey*, as far back as the 9th century BC: "These goat sausages sizzling here in the fire—we packed them with fat and blood to have for supper."

★ The English word sausage is derived from the Latin word *salsus*, which means to salt.

★ Sausages became known as 'bangers' during World War II because they were so filled with water that they exploded when cooked.

★ Natural sausage skins are made from the intestines of pigs, sheep or cows. Artificial skins are made from cellulose or collagen—often sourced from cow skin.

BAD SAUSAGES

With so many fabulous snags out there, why would anyone choose to buy those grim pink logs, commonly described by supermarkets as 'barbecue sausages'? I guess they need to label them, should shoppers mistake them for escapees from an adult toyshop.

Should you end up with some of these at your house—say, after a cheeky guest has brought them along to a barbecue and then eaten your good ones—you can jazz them up by coating in a mix of honey and Dijon mustard, or honey, tomato and soy sauce, and baking for 30 minutes or so until sticky and golden, and unrecognisably tasty.

PORK STIR-FRY

The trick to a successful stir-fry is preparation and coolness under pressure. If you can pull off a good one, then you're probably ready to tackle the Middle East situation.

Before you even fire up the wok, you need to get all your ingredients sorted—crushed, desseded, choppped and squeezed—just think of all those TV chefs who have little bowls of pre-prepared ingredients sitting in front of them.

When the cooking starts, it needs to go so fast that you won't have time to chop anything you've forgotten.

You can use any kind of noodles you like, but fresh, flat rice noodles are a doddle to prepare, as they only require a quick soak in boiling water.

This stir-fry, minus the noodles, can also be served on a pile of plain steamed rice, or in little lettuce cups as an appetiser.

Traditional stir-fries are light on meat and heavy on veggies. These should be cut small to speed up the cooking process—a mandolin is a boon, but you can also shred them very, very finely with a very, very sharp knife. Arrange the vegetables in bowls in order of their cooking time, with the longest-cooking vegetables first.

Heat the pan before you start cooking, and when you add the oil, give it a good tilt so the oil drizzles along the sides. Because of the shape of the wok, the ingredients don't just sit on the bottom so the sides need to be oiled as well.

SERVES 4

Ingredients

2 garlic cloves, crushed

1 large red chilli, deseeded and finely chopped

½ onion, finely diced

2 tablespoons vegetable or rice bran oil

500g finely minced pork

2 tablespoons fresh lime juice (or use tamarind paste)

6 Kaffir lime leaves, finely sliced

2 tablespoons palm sugar, grated (or use brown sugar)

2 tablespoons fish sauce

Method

1. Whiz the garlic, chilli and onion in a small food processor, or crush to a paste in a mortar and pestle.

2. Heat the oil in wok until almost smoking, then add the chilli-garlic paste and fry for a moment, until fragrant.

3. Crumble in the pork mince and fry for a few minutes until browned.

4. Add the lime juice, lime leaves, palm sugar and fish sauce, and allow to cook for a few minutes. Taste and adjust the flavourings to suit—it will be sweet and sour, spicy and salty all at the same time.

PORK STIR-FRY

400g fresh flat rice noodles, soaked in boiling water

1 carrot, shredded

1 red capsicum, shredded

1 cup fresh Thai basil leaves

1 cup fresh coriander leaves

½ cup Vietnamese hot mint

deep-fried shallots and unsalted peanuts, crushed, to serve

5. Drain the noodles, and slide into the wok along with the carrot and capsicum, and the fresh herbs.

6. Give the lot a good toss, remove from the heat and serve immediately, with crushed peanuts and deep-fried shallots sprinkled on top.

WHY A WOK?

With its high, sloping sides and rounded or flat bottom, the wok has been specifically designed for stir-frying. Unlike a standard frying pan, with a high-sided wok, you can happily stir and toss the food with ease without worrying about it winding up on the floor. The wok bottom also rests directly on the gas or electric element, allowing food to cook more quickly.

Woks distribute heat more evenly, and you also need less oil to cook, which is an advantage if you're fussed about that sort of thing.

Traditional woks came with two metal handles, making it easy to lift, but I actually prefer the long wooden handle seen on most modern woks. You don't need to use oven mitts for a start, and you can really get some leverage happening as you toss your food over the heat.

Go for carbon steel for preference, although you'll also find woks in aluminium, stainless steel and even copper.

BAD PORK STIR-FRY

Stir-fry novices often wonder why the end result is either gluggy, or sticks to the wok.

In the first case, it's usually because all the ingredients have been added at the same time—some will be overcooked, others not so much. Overloading the wok will also make the end result stodgy—you need room to toss it about so that every bit of the food gets its time close to the heat source. If in doubt, cook the stir-fry in two batches.

As for the second, adding oil to a cold wok is a surefire way of ending up with food stuck to the bottom. Heat the wok first, as described above, and don't forget the 'stir' part of stir-frying. It's called this for a reason.

ROAST PORK

Let's get one thing straight. The whole point of roast pork is the crackling. Get this right, and you'll have happy eaters; get it wrong, and you'll be drummed out of the kitchen.

Perfect crackling is golden brown, blistered and crunchy, but not so dry that it falls to powder in your mouth. It needs to crackle.

So how to achieve this? Lots of theories abound—salting the skin the night before and leaving it uncovered in the fridge. Rubbing with vinegar or lemon juice. Sacrificing your oldest child, ok, not really.

In my humble opinion, salt really is the answer—well, salt and the absence of moisture. So yes, leave it uncovered in the fridge overnight, first rubbing the rind with table salt to help draw out the moisture.

Just before you're ready to cook, after you've brought the whole thing up to room temperature, pat the joint dry with kitchen towel then oil it very lightly and rub in some more salt (a mix of powdery table salt and salt flakes for a nice crust) just before you slide it into the oven.

The crackling needs a blast of heat to start it off in the right direction—say 220°C (425°F)—then reduce the temperature so the meat finishes equal first.

For pork at its most succulent, cook it so there's still a hint of pink. While folklore and some over-zealous zealots have it that pork needs to be cooked all the way through, overcooking will make the meat tough and dry. Don't be scared of a little bit of pink, but to be absolutely sure, stick a thermometer into its middle and aim for a core temperature of 70-75°C (158-165°F). If you don't have a meat thermometer, stick a skewer into the middle. The juices will be running clear at this stage, even if the flesh itself is still a little bit rosy.

After removing your pork from the oven, cover the roasting pan with foil and leave it to rest for about 15 minutes before carving. This allows the juices to settle, so the flesh becomes more succulent.

SERVES 6

Ingredients

1.7kg boned loin of pork

1 tablespoon olive oil or olive oil cooking spray

2 teaspoons salt (a mixture of table salt and sea salt flakes)

PORK WITH CARAMELISED APPLE WEDGES

Method

1. Preheat your oven to 220°C (425°F). Using a sharp knife or, better yet, a Stanley knife, score the pork skin at 1cm intervals if the butcher hasn't already done this for you.

2. Roll up the pork into a neat log and tie with cooking string to secure. Spray the skin with oil and rub with the salt. Place the pork onto a rack in a large greased baking dish and roast for 30 minutes.

ROAST PORK

For the caramelised apple wedges

20g unsalted butter

3-4 apples (such as Golden Delicious or Granny Smith), cored and cut into wedges

50g caster sugar

balsamic vinegar

1 spring onion, trimmed and finely sliced

salt and black pepper

3. Reduce heat to 200°C (400°F). Roast for a further 50-60 minutes.

4. While the meat is cooking, melt the butter in a large frying pan. Toss the apples in the caster sugar and add to the pan when the butter starts foaming. Fry for 3-4 minutes on each side over medium heat until golden brown and caramelised. Add a splash of balsamic vinegar, the spring onion, and season to taste with salt and black pepper.

5. The pork should be ready now—check by testing if the juices run clear when you insert a skewer into the meat. Leave to rest for 10 minutes before carving. This also gives you the chance to give your crackling a final burst of heat if it's still looking a bit flabby (see below).

6. Once all the stars are aligned, remove the string from the pork, slice and serve with the apple wedges.

ON THE SIDE

Brighten up the plate with colourful root vegetables cut into 3cm chunks and lightly caramelised in the oven alongsde the roast. Carrots, sweet potatoes, pumpkin and spuds are all ideal candidates.

Simply chuck the lot into a separate roasting tray along with some quartered onions, whole garlic cloves and some olive oil, sprinkle with fresh herbs and leave to roast below the pork.

For something even more rustic, simply roast a head of garlic until soft, squeeze out the insides, then whizz with a couple of cans of cannellini beans (drained and warmed through), salt, pepper, a squeeze of lemon and a good slosh of olive oil.

BAD ROAST PORK

Soft rubbery crackling is the ultimate failure. It also shows that you don't care, as all you have to do to retrieve crackling that's underdone is peel it away from the meat and give it a good blast in a very hot oven by itself, or even under a grill (as a last resort). But you do need to keep an eye on it—it will have too much crunch (if that's possible) if it goes too far.

ROAST LAMB

With the exception of vegetarians and vegans, practically everyone loves a good roast of lamb—cooks included.

The main reason for this is that compared with beef and pork, lamb is a very forgiving roast and, unlike pork, there's no mission-critical need to get the crackling perfect (a classic 1.5kg roast takes 1 ½ hours for medium). Just remember:

- ⋆ Cold meat won't roast evenly, so bring the lamb to room temperature by taking it out of the fridge a couple of hours ahead of when you need to cook it.
- ⋆ The skin needs to be dry to crisp up, so remove any plastic wrapping and cover it with a tea towel while it comes to room temperature. Before roasting, rub the skin all over with salt for extra crunch.
- ⋆ You don't want the lamb to stew in its own juices, so either position it on a rack or on a layer of veggies in the roasting tin.

The veggies will also add flavour to the juices. In the British style, lamb's perfect match is rosemary, with its pine fragrance marrying beautifully with the sweet meat. Garlic too, goes beautifully with lamb, although lumps of garlic in the flesh are not to everyone's taste.

Other complementary seasonings for lamb include, oregano, marjoram, thyme, lemon zest, cumin, coriander, mint and garlic. To get a real depth of flavour into a standard roast, you can trim some of the fat before seasoning the lamb, then rub some chopped herbs evenly over the surface of the meat. Wrap the seasoned lamb tightly in plastic wrap and refrigerate it overnight so that the flavours begin to infuse the meat.

This recipe is for Greek-style slow-cooked lamb—even easier than the British-style roast, with hours of oven time turning the flesh tender enough to tear apart with a fork.

GREEK-STYLE SLOW-COOKED LAMB

SERVES 6

Ingredients

2kg leg or shoulder lamb

1 tablespoon olive oil

2 teaspoons sea salt flakes

4 garlic cloves, thickly sliced

fresh oregano sprigs

½ cup dry white wine

Method

1. Preheat the oven to 180°C (350°F). Place the lamb in a large roasting pan, drizzle with oil and sprinkle with salt.
2. Using a small, sharp knife, cut deep slits all over the surface of the lamb, inserting a sliver of garlic and oregano into each.
3. Splash the wine and stock around the lamb and cover the whole tray with aluminium foil.

ROAST LAMB

1½ cups stock—lamb ideally, but chicken or vegetable will do

2 red onions, peeled and quartered

12 Kipfler potatoes, halved lengthways

2 very ripe lemons, quartered, plus the juice of 1 more

1 cup Kalamata or other fleshy black olives

4. Cook in the preheated oven for 1 hour. Remove the tray from the oven and baste the meat with the pan juices. Scatter the onion, potato, lemon and olives into the pan, and replace the meat.

5. Pour the lemon juice over the crust of the lamb to give it an extra tang. Re-cover with the foil and roast for a further hour.

6. To make sure everything crisps up, you need to remove the foil now and continue roasting for another 30 minutes or so, until the lamb is golden brown and very tender.

7. Remove from the oven. Cover with foil and set aside for 15 minutes to rest.

8. Slice the lamb thickly, arrange on serving plates with the onion, potato and olives, and drizzle each serving with a tablespoon of the pan juices. Serve immediately.

CLASSIC ACCOMPANIMENTS

Roast potatoes (see page 64) and mint sauce or jelly are the standard partners for roast lamb.

Funnily enough, and in keeping with the Greek-style lamb recipe described here, anchovies marry beautifully with lamb too—poke fillets into slits in the flesh, or squish them into the gravy. Even anchovy-haters won't know they are there, and they add a wonderful savoury taste.

BAD ROAST LAMB

You can tell a hit from a miss the moment you look at the plate—bad roast lamb is grey and stringy. And while slow-roasted lamb won't have the same pinkness as regular roast lamb, what it loses in colour, it more than makes up for in flavour.

Bad roast lamb is also generally accompanied by gravy out of a packet. This is a shame because if you cook it in the same way as described here, you don't even have to make gravy because the juices themselves provide the perfect sauce.

SAUCES AND CONDIMENTS

BÉCHAMEL SAUCE 130
HOLLANDAISE SAUCE 132
VINAIGRETTE 134
PESTO 136
TAPENADE 138
MAYONNAISE 140
JAM 142
CUSTARD 144

CHAPTER 9

SAUCES AND CONDIMENTS

For all those who say that sauces and condiments aren't food—that they're the frippery around the edges, the finishing touch, the bit you can leave out—imagine scones without jam, eggs Benedict without the hollandaise, lasagne or cauliflower cheese without the perfect béchamel sauce.

Learn to cook these basics well, and you'll have built the foundation for a zillion new dishes, sweet and savoury alike.

BÉCHAMEL SAUCE

For such a bland-tasting liquid, béchamel, or white sauce, is an incredibly useful thing to have in your repertoire. It's not a dish in itself, and it's never a hero in the same way that hollandaise sauce steals the limelight whenever it appears, but all the same it plays a vital supporting role in lots of delicious dishes that you will want to cook time and time again.

Think of the perfect white sauce as a carrier of flavour—whether that means chunks of briny fish and prawns in a fish pie (see page 102) or sharp cheddar for your cauliflower cheese.

The white sauce should not draw attention to itself through lumps or a gluggy texture, but should be creamy, smooth and seasoned to perfection.

If you wish, you can add a subtle touch of flavour by infusing the warm milk with a bunch of herbs tied together with a bit of kitchen string, which makes them easier to remove. Traditionally, French chefs—yes, this recipe originated in France during the reign of Louis XIV in the 1650s—would sometimes flavour the sauce by adding an onion studded with cloves.

MAKES 200-400ML

Ingredients

200-400ml full-cream milk, depending on how thick you want your sauce to be—the less milk the thicker it will be

50g butter

50g plain flour

salt and black pepper

ground nutmeg

fresh herbs, a bay leaf, quarter onion, chunk of carrot all tied together with kitchen string (optional)

Method

1. In a saucepan, warm the milk gently and keep it at a slow simmer (don't let it boil) while you prepare the flour and butter paste.

2. On low heat, melt the butter in a second saucepan until it just begins to gently foam. Tip in the flour all at once and stir it through the butter. Let it cook for a minute or so, stirring all the while, then add a little of the milk and stir until the butter, flour and milk have formed a smooth paste.

3. Add the rest of the milk, about a third at a time, and stir, stir, stir until it all comes together and no lumps remain.

4. Cook for another few minutes, seasoning to taste with salt, pepper, a pinch of nutmeg and your bunch of herbs and veggies, if using.

WHEN TO USE YOUR PERFECTLY COOKED BÉCHAMEL SAUCE

* Having completed the third step of the method, turn the béchamel into a cheese sauce for cauliflower or other lightly cooked veggies by adding some sharp cheddar.
* As a key ingredient in dishes that require ingredients to be bound together (macaroni cheese, fish pie, croquettes, see page 84, 102, 36 respectively) and also in lasagna, where it helps moisten the pasta sheets and hold the rich, meaty layers together.
* Mix a thick béchamel sauce with some cooked and boned chicken, mixed cooked vegetables, herbs, salt and pepper, and a teaspoon of chicken stock powder. Pop into a pie dish, cover with a lid of puff pastry, and bake at 180°C (350°F) for about 45 minutes for an easy chicken pot pie.
* Add 2 or 3 teaspoons of grated onion or horseradish to the sauce and serve with salmon, meatloaf or fishcakes.
* Flavour with a tablespoon of tangy Dijon, hot English or seeded mustard (depending on your preference) and serve with good-quality cooked ham or pork cutlets.

BAD BÉCHAMEL SAUCE

Half the time, the problem lies in undercooking the sauce, so that it still has a nasty taste of flour. Take your time, stir well on low heat so that it doesn't brown or stick, and all will be well.

As for lumps, the trick here is to make sure your flour and butter paste is smooth before you add the bulk of the milk. This way, you'll reduce your chances of ending up with floury globules. But don't despair if, despite your best efforts, your sauce does end up with lumps—you can get rid of them manually with a stick mixer, in the food processor or even by pressing the sauce through a fine sieve.

If you overcook your sauce so that it becomes thick you can rescue it by simply adding a little more warm milk until you reach your desired consistency. And if you don't plan to use the sauce straight away, make sure you cover the top with cling film or else you'll end up with a plastic-like skin across the surface, which is another sign of bad béchamel.

SAUCES AND CONDIMENTS

HOLLANDAISE SAUCE

Good hollandaise sauce is a joy, bringing a touch of sunshine yellow and tangy lemon to all manner of dishes—from salmon and white fish to broccoli, artichoke hearts, eggs Benedict (see page 26 for perfect poached eggs) and steamed asparagus (see page 60).

One of the classic French sauces, hollandaise is made from an emulsion of egg yolks and butter, usually seasoned with lemon juice, and cooked over gentle heat. The secret is to keep the heat low so that the egg yolks don't curdle and to whisk, whisk, whisk until you think your wrist will drop off.

Hollandaise is like a buttery version of mayonnaise. It's the same theory—emulsion—but here, the oil comes from butter rather than olive oil. The sauce should be light yellow and opaque in appearance, and a smooth, creamy consistency. The flavour is rich and buttery, with a mild tang added by the lemon juice, yet not so strong as to overpower mildly flavoured foods like poached salmon or eggs.

SERVES 4

Ingredients

4 free-range egg yolks

3½ tablespoons lemon juice

ground white pepper (you don't want black flecks throughout the sauce)

1 tablespoon water

225g butter, melted

¼ teaspoon salt

Method

1. Partially fill the bottom of a double boiler with water (or use a metal bowl over a saucepan), making sure the water does not touch the top pan. Bring the water to a very gentle simmer.

2. In the top of the double boiler, whisk together the egg yolks, lemon juice, a pinch of white pepper and water. As the yolks begin to cook, you'll notice that the mixture starts to resist the whisk slightly more. It will become thick enough that it sort of coats the bottom of the bowl when it's tilted. Also, as you lift the whisk out of the mixture some of it will fall back into the bowl in ribbons. However, the main indication that the yolks are fully cooked is the presence of steam. The moment you see any steam coming out of the bowl, take it off of the heat—you don't want the eggs to start scrambling.

3. Now it's time to emulsify the eggs with the butter. Add the melted butter to the egg yolk mixture 1 or 2 tablespoons at a time, whisking furiously as you go.

4. If the hollandaise begins to get too thick, add 1 or 2 teaspoons of hot water. Continue whisking until all butter is incorporated. Whisk in the salt, then remove from the heat. Place a lid on the pan to keep the sauce warm until you are ready to serve.

PREPARE AHEAD AND IMPRESS YOUR GUESTS

If you want to look really flash the next time you have people round, stun them with some homemade hollandaise sauce. The good news is that you don't have to do it under the eagle eye of your guests, as hollandaise keeps perfectly well in the fridge for up to two weeks, as long as it is stored in a sealed jar.

To rewarm your perfect sauce (don't forget you'll have plenty of time to make sure it is perfect) pop it in the microwave on medium-low, stirring every 30 seconds, until it reaches the desired temperature.

Be careful not to overheat it or the sauce will split—that is, separate out into a thin oily stream and yellow curds. Not good.

BAD HOLLANDAISE SAUCE

There is a good reason hollandaise is considered notoriously difficult to make—because it is, at least if you do it properly. I should say now that there is a cheat's version that relies upon the use of a food processor and hot butter to slightly cook the egg yolks, but in my book the resulting sauce is not real hollandaise.

In essence, bad hollandaise—split hollandaise—results from letting the mix get too hot. Even experienced cooks can easily screw it up through a moment's inattention. What happens then is that the yolks become scrambled, which is fine if you're after lemony scrambled eggs, but not so great if you're aiming for a sauce. You'll know if your hollandaise has gone bad if it looks like processed cheese whip.

The key is to make sure that you keep the temperature low—it should be just a little bit warmer than body temperature. Stick your finger in to test the temperature as you go, but don't forget to keep whisking as you do.

If the sauce splits it is sometimes possible to recover it. Whisk together a new egg yolk with a tablespoon of cold water. While whisking, drizzle the bad sauce in very slowly. Return to the double boiler, heat gently and hopefully it all comes back together again. Sadly, I have to admit, this purported rescue remedy has never worked for me, but maybe you'll have better luck!

SAUCES AND CONDIMENTS

VINAIGRETTE

A vinaigrette, often referred to as French dressing, is most commonly used to bring out the flavour of fresh salad leaves (although it can also be used to dress other dishes, such as chicken, fish or vegetables), and is traditionally made from a simple emulsion of oil and vinegar (or another acid, such as lemon juice).

Simple, yes, but perfection lies in the ratio of the two key ingredients. As a rule of thumb, use four parts oil to one part of vinegar. If using lemon juice instead of vinegar, the ratio is more like two parts oil to one part lemon juice.

Once you have the basic vinaigrette recipe and technique down pat, feel free to experiment with different types of oils and vinegars. Quality red wine vinegar or sherry vinegar, verjuice, lemon juice or lime juice all make a great vinaigrette. For the oil, try also walnut, sunflower or avocado oils, or perhaps a subtly flavoured lemon-pressed olive oil. You might decide to steer clear of strongly flavoured vinegars, such as balsamic, and always remember to taste and adjust the quantities as you go.

It's also perfectly acceptable to add extra pizzazz with other flavourings—think mashed garlic, sliced spring onions, minced white onion, chopped herbs, capers, gherkins, diced anchovies, hard-boiled egg and mustards.

Be guided by the type of dish you plan on dressing—more strongly flavoured ingredients such as steamed cauliflower or peppery rocket will take a more robust combination of flavours, such as garlic and red wine vinegar. Roasted chicken goes well with a full-bodied balsamic vinaigrette, but for a delicate white fleshed fish you probably need something lighter—perhaps lemon juice, a shaving of lemon zest and some chopped dill or fresh coriander.

MAKES 300ML

Ingredients

240ml extra-virgin olive oil

60ml white wine vinegar

sea salt flakes and black pepper

Method

1. Whisk the oil and vinegar until a thick, creamy emulsion forms, then add the salt and pepper to taste. You can also pop the ingredients in a screw-top jar and shake well.

2. Dress your salad leaves with the vinaigrette just before serving, and be careful to tip out any excess dressing—you don't want the salad going soggy.

TIPS FOR PERFECTION

For best results, all your ingredients should be at room temperature when you begin. The cooler the oil, the more difficult it is to make an emulsion.

Once you've mixed things up, it's a good idea to let the flavors meld for a while, particularly if you've gone beyond the basic formula and introduced additional ingredients like minced onion, herbs and so on. Ideally, then, you'd prepare the vinaigrette in advance and let it sit at room temperature for a while.

Make sure the leaves have been thoroughly washed and dried before you attempt to dress the salad. Oil and water don't mix! A salad spinner can come in handy here.

Get your hands into the bowl when you dress the salad. You want each leaf to have been lightly caressed with the dressing—don't get too enthusiastic though, or you'll bruise the leaves.

If the vinaigrette has been stored in the fridge, make sure you bring it out and let it reach room temperature before using. Shake well to emulsify the dressing again and taste to make sure the seasoning is still right.

BAD VINAIGRETTE

Rubbish vinaigrette results from using crappy ingredients—cheap or rancid oil and vinegar—or from mixing great ingredients in the wrong proportions. Too much vinegar will not only make your mouth pucker up like a cat's bum, but will destroy the taste of the salad leaves themselves.

The flavour of your vinaigrette can also be ruined by using an aluminium bowl for mixing—the acid in the vinegar will react with the aluminium, producing a metallic flavour. Instead, whizz it in a blender, or use a glass or stainless steel bowl.

If all this seems like too much trouble, or your fellow diners all have wildly differing tastes, simply pop some bottles of great olive oil and vinegar on the table and allow people to dress their own salads. Each individual simply splashes the leaves with oil, then vinegar, and tosses the salad with a spoon and fork or salad tongs on their plate.

PESTO

Pesto, or more accurately pesto Genovese, developed like most great food items through plenty (basil and pine nuts) and initiative (adding the best olive oil, garlic and hard, granular cheese (parmesan and sometimes pecorino) for spunk, texture and masses of flavour.

Originating from the seaside city of Genoa in the Ligurian region of Italy, the name pesto derives from the Genovese word *pestâ*, which means to pound or crush. Making this pungent paste is a delight in so many ways—it uses energy, as you combine the ingredients in that ancient crusher, the mortar and pestle, and it fills the air with the most delicious, evocative aromas. For real joy, grab the bowl, put it in the front seat of the car and drive around the block. Freshly made pesto in the confines of the car sits with other great 'car aromas'—freshly ground coffee, hot pizza and pesto are my favourites!

It's an incredibly versatile flavouring sauce, dip and spread, and it is so motivating to know that all the muscle-power and hard work that goes into the preparation will have so many potential outcomes. Yes, you can make pesto in a whizzer, but it's boring and the fruit of your labour will taste so much better it you make pesto by hand.

MAKES 1 LARGE CUP

Ingredients

50g pine nuts or walnuts

1 teaspoon salt, preferably rock salt

2 teaspoons black peppercorns

1-3 cloves garlic, depending on your need for it and the strength of the clove (depends on season)

1½ cups extra-virgin olive oil

5 cups fresh basil leaves

200g parmesan or pecorino, grated

Method

1. Mix the nuts, salt, peppercorns, garlic and a little of the oil, and crush them in the mortar. It's a good idea to crush the garlic with the back of a heavy knife before you attack it with the pestle. If you haven't got a mortar, you can do all this with a kitchen hammer, but I bet you won't do it twice—it can get messy.

2. Add most of the basil leaves (leave ½ cup for later), a handful at a time and work the lot together, adding a little oil to assist the blending.

3. Add the parmesan and pound it all together.

4. Put the lot in a bowl and gradually add the rest of the oil, working the mixture with a wooden spoon. Add the rest of the basil. It won't keep for long, but if you cover the mixture with a thin layer of olive oil and store it in the fridge in a screw-top jar or airtight container it should last a week or so.

GREAT USES OF PESTO

Pasta is a natural partner for pesto as the heat of the cooked pasta brings out all the glorious flavours of the pesto. Try *trofie*, also hailing from Liguria, which is rolled by hand into little squiggly shapes. Failing that, any shape pasta is fine and a matter of personal preference. Pesto also goes well with ravioli—the Genoese opt for the veal and cheese stuffed variety.

Spread thickly on warm slices of toast and top with grilled sardines, or dollop on a homemade veggie pizza.

Use pesto as 'butter' in a sandwich of warm salmon chunks and peppery rocket, as a chunky salad dressing tossed with rocket leaves and chunks of gorgonzola, or toss through just-boiled baby potatoes.

BAD PESTO

It has always been the case that pesto has had variations, depending on climate, supply and local custom, but none of those can be considered in the same league as the real thing, pesto Genovese.

The French—or at least those from Provence—created a similar nut-free paste called *pistou*, which is a mix of basil, parsley, salt, grated cheese and crushed garlic. This, and other local variations (swapping pine nuts for walnuts or almonds, for example) are fine things to do, and are simply examples of using local initiative to get close to the real thing.

However, some modern cooks seem to think that anything that's old needs a lift to keep its place in the new world. Bosh, I say, but making variations of pesto seems to be *de rigueur* in second-tier eating houses. Bad pesto comes about when smarties decide that it's okay to replace basil with coriander or rocket and still insist on calling it pesto. One of the worst I've seen was to replace the pine nuts with peanut butter. Terrible. It's as close to pesto Genovese as a Kia is to a Rolls-Royce.

TAPENADE

In case you've never come across tapenade, it's a traditional Provençal paste made with olives, capers and herbs, which are pounded, puréed or finely chopped and mixed together with a generous slosh of olive oil. Some, including myself, deviate from the purist's version and add anchovies and garlic to the mix. Try both.

The addition of anchovies and garlic will make you tapenade sharper, more pungent, saltier and with more layers of flavour. The name tapenade, by the way, comes from the Provençal word for capers, *tapenas*.

Tapenade is extremely versatile and can be used in a number of ways, rather than just as a dip or spread. Packing a flavoursome punch, it's like the bruiser of the sauce world, giving a real kick in the pants to whatever it comes into contact with. Hollandaise sauce, on the other hand, gives more of a delicate hug to ingredients like fish, vegetables and eggs.

As always, a good tapenade relies upon the quality of the ingredients and the cook's competent use of them. Grab the best olives you can get your hands on—green ones are lighter in flavour, while black ones have a stronger, earthier taste. Ready-pitted olives might make life easier, but sometimes they lack flavour.

Make sure your capers are well rinsed of their salt or brine, and dry them well with kitchen towel before using them. Channel the south of France and use *herbes de Provence*—a mix of the herbs including basil, fennel seed, lavender, marjoram, rosemary, sage and thyme—available prepackaged from most supermarkets. Make this tapenade at least one day before you intend to serve it, so the flavours have time to develop.

MAKES 1 LARGE CUP

Ingredients

275g olives

3 tablespoons capers, well drained and dried

generous pinch fresh thyme or *herbes de Provence*

60ml extra-virgin olive oil

1 clove of garlic, crushed

3 anchovies

Method

1. Cut, scrape or pinch off the flesh from the olives and discard the stones.

2. Whizz up the olives, capers and herbs with a stick blender, in a food processor or pound to a mush in a large mortar and pestle. Add the olive oil, garlic and anchovies, and whizz until it reaches your desired consistency. A food processor is fast, but you need to be light-fingered on the pulse button if you want chunks rather than a really fine paste.

3. Dip a finger in and taste. If you want more sharpness, add a few more capers; more unctuousness, a dash more oil.

4. You can keep the tapenade stored in the refrigerator covered by a ½cm-deep layer of olive oil to preserve it, where it will keep for several months.

GREAT WAYS WITH TAPENADE

So what do you do with the stuff, aside from smearing it on artisan bread, pita, crostini or crackers? Almost anything you eat, apart from perhaps ice cream, will benefit from the addition of tapenade:

- Dollop next to plainly cooked fish, lamb or poultry.
- Use it as a sandwich spread, instead of mustard or mayo.
- Spread a thin layer between the skin and the flesh of a chicken before roasting.
- Mash up hard-boiled eggs with a spoonful of tapenade and serve on toast.
- Fold some into an omelette with a round of goats' cheese.
- Stir tapenade into plain rice, or add to a tomato sauce destined for a plate of piping-hot pasta.
- Serve as a dip with raw vegetables or breadsticks, or use it to flavour a plain vinaigrette.

BAD TAPENADE

Just as some food freaks believe that it's possible to improve on classic pesto, others screw around with tapenade by adding all sorts of ingredients. Some recipes don't even contain any capers—for which the dish is named—and instead use anything from figs to eggplant, tuna, mayo, egg, green peppers, apples, cranberries, pistachios, or even shiitake mushrooms. Don't be fooled—this is not tapenade—it's spread.

Aside from your choice of ingredients, there's little you can do to stuff up tapenade. Even the texture doesn't really matter: it can be coarsely chopped, smooth, chunky, runny or thick, depending on your elbow power or how long you process it for. The resulting mixture can be thinned with olive oil to any consistency you desire. Of course, tapenade can be store bought, but it beats me why you want to, when this dish can be whipped up in minutes with the aid of a food processor—or rather longer if you use a mortar and pestle. It also keeps for yonks in the fridge so is a great standby if you want to add some pizzazz to an otherwise simple dish.

MAYONNAISE

Once you've mastered the art of homemade mayonnaise, you can can save your cents and never bother with the stuff out of a jar again. There is just no comparison: as well as being a rich, egg-yolk yellow rather than a sickly white, the homemade version is less sugary, made with only natural ingredients and completely lacking in any chemical aftertaste.

However weird it might sound, the key to a successful mayonnaise is making sure that every droplet of oil is thoroughly whisked in before adding the next drop. This is the do-or-die moment, where you need to take it very slowly, or risk the mayonnaise curdling.

But don't worry—it won't take you forever, because after a few minutes, once the critical point has passed and the mayonnaise has begun to thicken, you can then begin pouring the oil in a thin but steady stream. A plastic squeeze bottle with a very small nozzle works brilliantly to help regulate the flow of oil.

The lazy cook's alternative—and by far my preferred way—is to do the whole lot in the food processor or with a stick blender, letting the machine do all the hard whisking work, while you concentrate on dribbling the oil down the funnel drop by drop.

Once you have a few successful batches under your belt, you can start experimenting with different flavours. Try substituting lime juice for lemon juice, or you might find you prefer the sharper tang of vinegar. Add a few pinches of cayenne pepper for a fiery punch, capers, lemon rind and gherkins for tartare sauce, or mixed herbs for an authentic rustic taste. Whatever your palate, once you've learnt how to make mayonnaise you'll never look at those aneamic imitations on the supermarket shelves again.

MAYONNAISE

MAKES 1½ CUPS

Ingredients

2 free-range egg yolks—make sure they're really fresh

1 teaspoon Dijon mustard

salt and black pepper

300ml olive oil, or a mix of olive oil and vegetable or grapeseed oil, for a lighter flavour

1 tablespoon fresh lemon juice, or to taste

Method

1. Sit a large bowl on a tea towel to stop it moving about or worse, slipping off the bench and onto the floor.

2. Put the egg yolks into the bowl with the Dijon mustard, a little seasoning and half the lemon juice. Whisk well until smooth.

3. With your free hand, gradually add the olive oil, drop by drop, until the mix begins to thicken. At this stage, you can start pouring it, in a slow, steady stream, whisking all the time. You should have a smooth, thick mayonnaise that stands in peaks, a bit like whipped cream.

4. Add some more lemon juice and seasoning to taste and briefly whisk. If the mixture is too thick, whisk in a few drops of warm water to give a good consistency.

POSH MAYONNAISE OR AIOLI

Basically, aioli is mayonnaise tarted up with the addition of raw garlic (or roasted, mashed garlic for a sweeter, nuttier flavour). Simply add 4 large cloves of garlic, pounded well with a mortar and pestle, to the egg yolks at the start of the traditional mayonnaise recipe and omit the lemon juice.

This lovely, creamy, garlicky dip is best served immediately and goes fantastically well with all kinds of fish, cooked all kinds of ways, as well as barbecued octopus, meat, vegetables and fried potatoes.

BAD MAYONNAISE

Mayonnaise can be ruined by using olive oil that is very strongly flavoured, so always opt for a light, fruity oil that allows the flavour of the fresh lemon to shine through.

Mayonnaise will curdle if you add the oil too quickly at the beginning. But if that happens, don't despair. All you need to do is put a fresh egg yolk into a clean basin, add the curdled mixture to it (drop by drop), then blithely continue adding the rest of the oil as though nothing happened. The fresh yolk will re-emulsify your mayonnaise.

SAUCES AND CONDIMENTS

#

Making your own strawberry jam is surprisingly easy and satisfying, especially if you've chanced upon fruit going cheap at the market, or visited a pick-your-own farm.

All you need are some just-ripe, unblemished berries and a little time up your sleeve. And, of course, a good scone recipe (see page 162) just crying our for lashings of homemade jam and clotted cream.

Choose barely ripe berries rather than fully ripe ones, as these are higher in pectin—the stuff that helps jam set. Strawberries are relatively low in pectin—as are bananas, pineapples and peaches—so add some lemon juice to lend a helping hand.

It is important to wash and dry the fruit before hulling and chopping it, otherwise it will absorb too much water. And follow the proportions of sugar and fruit—too much sugar will lend your jam a gritty feeling.

Use a large, enamelled cast-iron or stainless steel saucepan with lots of room for the jam to bubble away and be aware the aluminium pans can change the colour of the fruit. Finally, make sure the sugar has completely dissolved before you bring the jam to the boil. Simmering the sugar and fruit slowly also helps to extract the fruit's natural pectin.

MAKES 6 LARGE JARS

Ingredients

3kg strawberries, washed, dried, then hulled and halved

juice of 2 lemons

3kg sugar

Method

1. Wash and sterilise the jars and lids (you can do this in the dishwasher, but take care not to touch inside the jars when removing them). Dry thoroughly in an oven set to a low temperature.

2. Place the strawberries, lemon juice and sugar in a large saucepan. Heat over low heat and simmer gently, stirring all the while, until the sugar dissolves.

3. Turn the heat up to medium and boil the mixture for 10 minutes, stirring occasionally, until the fruit has mostly turned to mush then do the 'wrinkle test' (see Ready, Test, Set). If the jam doesn't wrinkle the first time, keep boiling it for another 5 minutes and then test again on another cold plate.

4. If the jam is ready, remove saucepan from the heat, remove any scum from the surface with a spoon and let it sit for 10 minutes or until the edges of the jam set slightly. This prevents the fruit rising to the top when put into the jars.

5. Stir the jam then pour into the warm jars—filling to the top to allow for shrinkage. Seal tightly straight away to keep out the air. The jam will keep for up to a year in a cool, dark place; after opening, store it in the fridge, where it will keep for about three months.

READY, TEST, SET

There are two simple ways to test for setting point. Easiest of all, you can test for temperature with a sugar thermometer, as the jam is ready at 108°C (226°F). If you don't have a thermometer, you can use the 'wrinkle test'. Simply drop a spoonful of the jam onto a saucer that has been chilled in the freezer and leave to cool for a moment. If it wrinkles when you push it with your finger, then it's done. If not, boil it for another 5 or 10 minutes and then check again.

BAD JAM

You'll know you've failed your jam class if you open a jar only to discover more of a syrup than a wibbly-wobbly jelly. This means that your jam did not reach setting point before you finished cooking it.

Bad jam is also jam that's been overcooked, or allowed to catch on the bottom of the saucepan. Once this happens, a burnt tang will seep through the whole mix. Throw it out and start again.

Jam can also go mouldy in the jar should you not have sterilised your equipment properly, or sealed the jars tightly enough. In this case, you may end up with bacteria or mould spores feeding off your precious jam. This will cause the top layer of the jam to go brown or even green, and the whole lot will smell and taste bad. Toss it. Mould is also a danger for jars that have been opened, which is why it's best to keep jam in the fridge once you've popped its top.

CUSTARD

Made from a mix of eggs, sugar and milk, creamy homemade custard is one of the most useful basics at the cook's fingertips. Sometimes flavoured with ingredients such as vanilla beans, orange, brandy or chocolate, custard is great on its own—both hot or cold—and also plays the starring role in sweet treats such as crème caramel, crème brûlée, trifle and as a base for ice cream. You can also mix it with shards of meringue (see page 174) or fresh fruit; bananas and custard are a perfect pairing.

Basically, there are two ways of making custard: stirring and baking. Stirred custards are cooked on the stovetop in a saucepan, and involve you stirring until your arm aches and the liquid becomes thick and creamy. Baked custards, on the other hand, are simply popped into a water bath and slipped into the oven to cook until set—this involves far less elbow grease, but results in an entirely different consistency (see Brilliant Baked Custard).

The trick to cooking custard well—without lumps and without it curdling—is to keep the temperature low and to make sure the liquid is constantly moving across the warm bottom of the saucepan. Eggs have a delicate structure and can separate or become tough and rubbery if they are cooked at too high a temperature. If you have a kitchen thermometer at hand, the liquid needs to stay below 80°C (175°C) throughout the cooking process. Adding a big pinch of cornflour to the eggs when you whisk them helps the mixture hang together without splitting, but isn't essential if you take care. It's also a good idea to strain the custard through a sieve to remove any eggy clumps before serving.

MAKES 1 ½ CUPS

Ingredients

2 cups full-cream milk

1 vanilla bean (or 1 teaspoon vanilla essence or paste)

4 free-range egg yolks

⅓ cup caster sugar

large pinch of cornflour (optional)

Method

1. Pour the milk into a small saucepan. Using a sharp knife, split the vanilla bean in half lengthways and scrape out the little black seeds. Add the bean and seeds to the milk and cook over medium heat, stirring constantly, for 5 minutes or until hot (do not allow to boil). Remove the saucepan from the heat and stand covered for 10 minutes. This allows the vanilla bean and seeds to do their stuff and the milk to cool slightly so that it doesn't scramble the eggs.

2. Whisk the egg yolks and sugar (and cornflour if using) in a bowl until thick and pale yellow in colour. Remove the vanilla bean from the milk then pour the warm vanilla milk over the egg yolk mixture, whisking constantly. (Don't discard the vanilla bean, but rinse and dry it, then add to your sugar canister to infuse the crystals with a lovely vanilla aroma).

3. Rinse the milk pan (this ensures that no bits of skin will end up in your custard) and return the lot to the saucepan over low heat. Cook, stirring constantly, for 15 to 20 minutes or until the custard thickens enough to coat the back of a metal spoon. You should be able to draw a line through the custard on the back of the spoon. Again, whatever you do, don't let the custard boil or it will curdle.

4. Serve the custard warm or cold, but if not using immediately, make sure to cover with clingfilm to prevent a skin forming. Homemade custard keeps in the fridge for a couple of days.

BRILLIANT BAKED CUSTARD

By cooking in a water bath (in a roasting pan), you help protect the custard from the hot metal base of the saucepan, preventing the liquid from overheating and separating. Lining the base of the roasting pan with a clean tea towel also helps. Place individual ramekins on top of this, and divide the custard mixture (as in recipe above) between them. Sprinkle with a pinch of freshly grated nutmeg.

Pour boiling water into the pan to reach halfway up the sides of the ramekins, then simply bake at 160°C (320°F) until the custards are just set. This will take about an hour, for ¾-cup capacity ramekins. To test if the custard is cooked, insert a knife in the centre. If the knife comes out clean, or with just a little softly set custard clinging to it, it's ready. The custard will continue to cook when removed from the oven so don't let it overcook or it will start to separate. Another sign of overcooking is tiny bubbles throughout the custard. It will still be perfectly edible but slightly grainy in texture.

BAD CUSTARD

There's a very good reason why so many people reach for a tin of custard powder, or a carton of ready-made from the dairy section of the supermarket: custard is a temperamental beast. The millisecond you take your eye off the pan, it can curdle, split or turn to scrambled eggs. Like most of the good things in life, custard requires attention, a degree of caution—and a lot of loving stirring.

If the worst does happen, and your custard curdles, there is one rescue remedy you can try before you feed it to the dog. Remove it from the heat immediately, run a sinkful of ice-cold water, and plunge the saucepan into this. Whisk like fury with a balloon whisk, and hopefully it will come back together. If not, start again.

You'll also need to start again should the custard catch on the bottom. There's simply no way to disguise the burnt taste, no matter how much brandy you pour in. On the other hand, if you have a minor mishap, like forgetting to cover the custard so that a skin forms on top, simply scoop it off with a metal spoon. The stuff underneath is perfectly good.

DESSERTS AND BAKING

SHORTCRUST PASTRY 148
LEMON TART 150
TRIFLE 152
SPONGE 154
APPLE PIE 156
FRUIT CRUMBLE 158
PEACH MELBA 160
SCONES 162
BERRY TART 164
BISCUITS 166
ICE CREAM 168
BROWNIES 170
CUPCAKES 172
MERINGUES 174
PAVLOVA 176
CHOCOLATE FUDGE CAKE 178
BREAD 180

CHAPTER 10

DESSERTS AND BAKING

Pudding, afters, sweets, dessert… whatever you call it, it's often the most anticipated part of a meal. There's even a recognised bit of the anatomy (thought to reside in the brain), that's commonly known as 'pudding stomach'. After a large main meal has been consumed, carriers of the pudding stomach gene are suddenly capable of finding room for dessert.

Baking is something that every cuisine and culture around the world shares. But it's no dark art, just physics, and there are some simple rules and ratios that you need to apply in order to end up with the best result. Whether it's bread or meringues, there's no substitute for experience. Get to know your oven, get to know your ingredients and practice until you get it right. Your friends will love you for it.

SHORTCRUST PASTRY

Perfect shortcrust pastry is buttery and crumbly, and the perfect base for making all sorts of pies and tarts. The richness comes from the proportion of flour to butter, and the addition of egg. It's dead easy to make—particularly if you just chuck it in the food processor—but there are a couple of tips to making it work every time.

First of all, make sure to stick religiously to the quantities and to only use cold butter. Warm butter will soon melt into the flour and the pastry is likely to tear when you roll it out. If the butter is too cold though, crumbling it into the flour will take forever.

Be aware that the amount of water needed to bring the dry ingredients together can vary, depending on how hot and humid it is. You'll need to build in some time for resting and chilling the dough, too. This makes it easier to work with.

The trickiest part is rolling out the pastry. In order for it to roll out smoothly, without sticking or tearing, it has to be at the right temperature. If it's too cold, it will tear (and you'll need all your strength to roll it out); too warm and it will stick like chewing gum. You'll soon get the feel for it with practice.

Shortcrust pastry can also be flavoured to complement whatever filling you are planning on making: think cinnamon to match a rich chocolate centre, lemon zest for a lemon tart, or vanilla seeds. A pinch of nutmeg or cocoa powder is great, too. Just don't go overboard…

Once you've mastered sweet shortcrust pastry, there are million recipes at your fingertips, a few of which are included on the following pages. Think apple pie, studded with cloves, lemon tart, a glistening berry tart, Bakewell tart, Mississippi mud pie, pecan pie and treacle tart, just for starters. You can also adapt the recipe for savoury pies and tarts by simply omitting the sugar and egg, and increasing the amount of water to about ¼ cup—more or less, depending on the weather and how quickly the dough comes together.

SHORTCRUST PASTRY

MAKES ENOUGH PASTRY FOR 1 X 23CM TART

Ingredients

200g flour, sifted

pinch of salt

1 tablespoon sugar

125g butter

1 free-range egg

2 teaspoons cold water

Method

1. Mix the flour, salt and sugar together in a large basin. Grate the butter over the top and work into the flour with your fingertips until it resembles breadcrumbs. Alternatively, you can plop the lot in a food processor and whiz until crumbly.

2. Mix the egg and water together and add to the crumble mix. Use a knife to bring it all together into a smooth dough. Again, you can do this in the food processor, but be careful to stop the machine as soon as the dough forms a large lump.

3. Scoop the dough out on to a sheet of clingfilm, wrap and chill in the fridge for at least 1 hour.

4. Remove from the fridge and roll out to the desired shape.

ROLLING, ROLLING, ROLLING

Make sure your work surface is totally clean and well dusted with flour before beginning to roll. You should never stretch the pastry while rolling—just turn it around, give it a pat with floured hands and give it another roll.

When you have a pastry disc the right size for your baking tin, slide it between two sheets of greaseproof paper and refrigerate for thirty minutes, before trimming to a neat shape and easing it into the greased pie or tart tin.

BAD SHORTCRUST PASTRY

Tough pastry is the sign of an over-anxious cook—a cook who fusses around with the pastry in an attempt to get it perfect. The problem is, the more you touch the pastry, the greater the likelihood that the butter will melt and that the end result will be chewy rather than light and crumbly. A good tip is to make your hands as cold as possible, by running them under cold water for as long as you can bear. Dry them carefully before you touch the pastry.

And while it's important to work with confidence and a degree of speed, pastry can also be ruined by rushing the process. Shortcrust pastry is relatively fragile, and handles best when chilled. This time hanging around in the fridge also allows the gluten in the flour to expand—which gives it its elasticity—so don't cut corners, no matter how harassed you might be.

LEMON TART

In my book, the perfect lemon tart has a crispy, sweet base that dissolves in your mouth and a light-as-air lemony filling. To achieve this, it's important to start with a shortcrust pastry recipe you know will do the job, and to make sure that the lemon filling has the perfect blend of sweetness and acidity.

Don't follow the recipe blindly, but make sure to taste it every time. Some lemons, depending on their state of ripeness, will offer up more juice than others, and the acidity of the juice will depend on the variety. I'm not going to say you must use a particular variety—who knows what you may have growing in your backyard—but instead to taste, taste, taste along the way. You want the lemon flavour strong enough to sing on your taste buds, not so sour that you purse your lips. Remember that thin-skinned lemons at room temperature will yield the most juice; cold thick-skinned ones, the maximum amount of zest.

The recipe here gets an extra kick from lemon zest, but you can also top your tart with very finely sliced lemons just before the end of cooking time—when the filling is almost set and the slices won't sink to the bottom. The final product can also be dressed up with a dusting of icing sugar, or a tumble of berries, but to my mind this is overkill, as it can screw up the delicate balance of flavours you've worked so hard to achieve.

SERVES 12

Ingredients

1 quantity shortcrust pastry (see page 148)

6 eggs

1½ cups caster sugar

juice and finely grated zest of 3 large lemons

⅔ cup orange juice (freshly squeezed, please)

3 tablespoons unsalted butter, melted

Method

1. Preheat the oven to 180°C (350°F) and prepare the pastry shell, as per the instructions for the berry tart on page 164.

2. Remove the shell from the oven and allow it to cool. You can prepare the shell ahead of time, then simply bake the filling on the day you intend serving.

3. When you are ready to make your filling, preheat the oven to 160°C (320°F).

4. For the filling, beat together the eggs and sugar until pale and light in colour. Carefully add the lemon zest, juices and melted butter. Stir well.

5. Pour the lemony liquid into the shell and bake for about 20 minutes until the filling is just set and starting to turn golden. Remove from the oven and allow to cool—still in its tin—on a wire rack. Then refrigerate. Serve cold, ideally with a lovely rich sticky wine.

TART TRANSFORMATION

The most common variation on a lemon tart is the pretty-as-a-picture lemon meringue pie. For this, simply cook the tart as described here, then cover with a billowing cloud of meringue. Simply beat 4 egg whites in a clean bowl until foamy, add ½ teaspoon cream of tartar and continue beating until soft peaks form. Gradually add ½ cup caster sugar and continue beating until the peaks become stiff.

Dollop the meringue mix all over the top of the tart, starting at the outside and making sure that it comes right up to the crust. With the back of your spoon, lightly press down on the meringue to make sure there are no air pockets and that the lemon curd is completely covered. Bake in a 160°C (320°F) oven for 10 minutes or until lightly golden.

BAD LEMON TART

Lemon tart is one of those dishes that bad cooks insist upon trying to improve. Steer clear of tragic reinventions such as polenta crusts and any kind of filling that involves cornflour. Sure this will help it set, but you'll end up with a gluggy, floury taste that no amount of sugar or lemon will disguise. Be sure too, to give the tart enough time in the oven to set. It should be gently wobbly, but certainly not liquid.

And beware of trying to do anything with your tart until it is totally cold. Even the most perfect tart will ooze should you attempt to cut it while still hot. It needs to be left in its dish and refrigerated until very cold—it's the perfect end to a dinner party, as it has to be done well ahead of time.

Of course, there's always a chance the pastry will crumble as you remove it from the tin—even when cold. To avoid this, use a loose-bottomed flan tin and make sure the sides are well greased. To remove the shell from the tin, simply pop the whole thing on top of an upside down tea cup or ramekin, and press down lightly on the edge of the pan. Magically, the shell will arise from the pan. Or that's the theory. You can also use your hand, as described in the berry tart on page 164.

TRIFLE

Rather than being a frippery or trivial thing—as the word trifle also means—a traditional English trifle is a serious object of desire (and calories!). Essentially, it's a soft mound of sponge cake soaked in alcohol, layered with berries, custard and cream.

The trifle has been a favourite for centuries, with the first-known recipe appearing in a medieval cookbook called *The Good Huswife's Jewell* by Thomas Dawson in 1596. However, that recipe produces a thick cream, flavoured with sugar, ginger and rosewater, and is more similar to what we think of today as a fool or syllabub. It wasn't until some thrifty soul added alcohol-soaked stale bread and leftover custard some 60 years later that the trifle as we know it was born.

Unsurprisingly, the Scots and Irish both added lots more alcohol, and ended up with both whim-wham (basically alcoholic cream) and tipsy cake (a polite term to describe an alcoholic cake). Meanwhile, the Italians created their own versions too: *zuppa Inglese* (English soup) and tiramisu, while the French dubbed theirs *mousse à l'Anglaise*. The recipe below is for a simply delicious English raspberry trifle.

SERVES ABOUT 6

Ingredients

200g sponge cake (see page 154)

½–1 cup sweet wine (for example Vin Santo), sherry or brandy—see Trifle Tricks

1 cup thickened cream

1 cup custard (see page 144)

300g fresh or frozen raspberries, mashed or puréed and thinned with a little orange juice until of a pouring consistency

extra berries, to decorate

Method

1. Crumble your sponge cake into lumps and pour over enough alcohol to soak it thoroughly.

2. Whisk the cream in a separate bowl until it forms soft folds and kind of plops off a spoon without any help. You don't want it to be completely liquid, nor too stiff. Gently fold half of this into another bowl containing the custard.

3. Drizzle the raspberry purée over the sponge cake, then spoon the custard-cream mix over the top of this. Don't be too pedantic about making the layers neat—you should end up with rough puddles of fruit and custard above the sponge.

4. Top with the reserved whipped cream and strew with the extra berries, and perhaps a final swirl of raspberry purée. Refrigerate for at least 3 hours, or overnight, before serving.

TRIFLE TRICKS

You can make the sponge cake (page 154) and custard (page 144) up to two days ahead, then simply assemble on the day you are going to eat it. However, you don't have time to make a sponge, then consider using sponge finger biscuits (*savoiardi*) or macaroons instead. These have the advantage of being easily cut into small shapes so that you can serve trifle in individual glasses. They also store perfectly well in the pantry, so you can whip up a trifle without too much hassle. As for the custard, the ready-made stuff from the chiller cabinet would do if you are time pressed.

And don't be afraid to experiment—angelica (acid-green crystallised or candied strips) and glacé cherries formed the traditional topping, but you can also use shaved chocolate, fresh fruit, crushed sweet biscuits, or almond slivers, to name but a few choices. As for the fruit, you can either use fresh fruit (berries, peaches, pears, mango), a purée (raspberry, strawberry, blackberry), jam or preserves, or any combination of these.

BAD TRIFLE

Now it's almost impossible to screw up something as simple as trifle, but believe me, an overly heavy hand with the alcohol will do it. It's dessert, after all, not a booze-up. I've also been served trifle made with creamy liqueurs such as Kahlua and Crème de Banane, but the end result was more of a cocktail with fruity lumps in it. More acceptable alternatives include sweet sherry, sweet white wine, rum, Grand Marnier, Amaretto and Frangelico. Be aware too that the amount of alcohol you'll need depends on how much liquid the cake absorbs—a sponge that is more than a day old will absorb more alcohol than a freshly made one. Jelly is a no-no in my book—nasty slimy stuff at the best of times.

Even with the right ingredients in the right proportion, you can do your trifle a disservice by not leaving enough time for the flavours to mingle. Luckily, trifles tend to be served at festive gatherings, so it's kind of handy to know that you can have the dessert prepared and in the fridge up to 24 hours beforehand.

And yes, presentation is also important. There's no point hiding all the glorious layers inside an opaque serving bowl, so use your most attractive glass or crystal bowl so guests can ooh and aah in anticipation.

SPONGE

A good cake is always a crowd pleaser—what's not to like about jam and cream sandwiched between two feathery slices of sponge? Sponges can seem intimidating to the uninitiated baker, but practically anyone can make a successful sponge if they understand the secret ingredient: air.

You need to get as much air in the mix as possible, every step of the way. Start by sifting your flour two or three times to aerate it and get rid of any lumps.

Make sure you use a non-plastic bowl for beating the eggs, or they won't get as fluffy as you need them to be. Then when you're actually beating the mixture, first beat on high to create lots of air pockets, then drop the speed back to medium and continue beating. You'll know it's ready for the flour when you can draw a figure of eight on the surface without it sinking back into the mixture straight away. Don't rush as this can take a while.

When adding the flour, use a large metal spoon to gently fold the mixture together. Don't use a wooden spoon as this will pop the air bubbles, and definitely don't beat it. Remember, the lighter and airier the mix is, the fluffier the end result.

Aside from the traditional strawberries and cream of a Victoria sponge (see Classic Sponge Presentation), you can fill your perfect cake with any sweet spread—lemon curd, cream mixed with raspberries or poached fruit, or whipped buttercream icing (see page 172) flavoured with orange, chocolate or even coffee.

MAKES 1 X 20CM CAKE

Ingredients

4 free-range eggs (55-60g), at room temperature

salt

¾ cup caster sugar

1 cup self-raising flour

2 tablespoons full-cream milk

2 tablespoons water

1 dessertspoon butter, melted

Method

1. Preheat oven to 180°C (350°F). Lightly grease 2 x 20cm sandwich tins and dust them with flour, shaking off any excess powder.

2. Crack the whole eggs into a bowl, add a pinch of salt and beat until they're light yellow and frothy.

3. Add the sugar a little at a time, beating as you go. After about 5 or 6 minutes, do the 'figure of 8' test (as above). This is just a practice run—generally it takes about 8 minutes to reach the right consistency, depending on your beaters.

4. Sift the flour into a bowl. Mix the milk, water and melted butter together. Then add the flour to the egg and sugar mixture, incorporating this gently with a whisk until combined. Dribble in the liquid mix as you are doing this.

5. Divide the mixture between the 2 tins—you can weigh them both to make sure they are exactly the same size if you're feeling fussy. Before placing the cake tins in the oven, tap each tin on the counter several times to pop any air bubbles on the top.

6. After 15 minutes in the oven, check your sponge. The cake is ready when it starts to pull away from the side of the tin and bounces back when you poke it lightly in the centre.

7. Once cooked, immediately turn the cakes onto a cake rack covered with a clean tea towel. Gently does it. Cover with another tea towel and leave to cool for about 30 minutes.

8. Then assemble your sponge sandwich with your choice of filling and serve to applause. Sponges are best eaten on the day they are made so don't hold back.

CLASSIC SPONGE PRESENTATION

The classic sponge is sometimes also known as a Victoria sponge, after Queen Victoria and, judging by her portraits, it's easy to believe she feasted on them regularly. Here, two cakes are layered together with jam and lightly whipped cream, then given a good dusting of icing sugar.

For the best results, pick the ugliest sponge to go on the bottom and place it on your serving plate. If it's a little rounded on top, simply trim it with a sharp knife so that it's perfectly flat. Smear over a nice thick layer of warmed jam (and some hulled and sliced strawberries if you're feeling flash) then top with a layer of cream that's been whipped to soft peaks.

Pop the second cake on top, making sure that its pretty side is facing up, and dust the whole confection with sifted icing sugar.

BAD SPONGE

A sponge that sinks in the middle is definitely not what you're after. If you've followed the steps above, your mixture will be perfectly light, but there are still a couple of traps for young players.

First of all, you need to get the mixture into the oven quick smart. The longer you leave the mixture sitting around, the more it will subside. Secondly, don't be tempted to open the oven door while your sponge cake is baking—the drop in temperature will cause it to sag in the centre. Leave it the full 15 minutes before testing.

The sponge should be done somewhere between 15 and 20 minutes, depending on your oven. The quicker it cooks, the finer the texture will be, which is what you're after. Knowing your oven is the key, so practice before you plan to show off your sponge skills.

APPLE PIE

The aroma of an apple pie baking takes some beating, particularly on a cold winter's night when you're in need of comfort food and there are months to go before there's any chance you'll be having to (horror of horrors) bare your body on the beach.

The key to getting the perfect pie doesn't just lie in the pastry (see the shortcrust pastry recipe on page 148) but in the apple and how it's cooked. Many recipes simply tell you to pile the raw pastry shell full of raw apple, and let both apple and pastry cook at the same time. But by cooking the apple first, you'll concentrate the flavours of the apple and spices, and reduce the amount of liquid. This helps prevent the pie bottom from going soggy and falling apart as you try to serve it up.

Vanilla ice cream, custard or plain cream are the traditional accompaniments, though some swear by a slice of sharp cheddar cheese.

SERVES 6-8

Ingredients

1 quantity shortcrust pastry (see page 148)

For the filling

30g unsalted butter

2-3 cinnamon sticks, broken into large pieces

6-8 cloves

100g sugar

1kg tart green apples (Bramley or similar), peeled, cored and cut into chunks

egg white, lightly whisked, for brushing the pie lid

caster sugar, to dust

Method

1. Preheat oven to 180°C (350°F) and lightly grease a 25cm pie dish.

2. Divide the pastry into 2 lumps. On a lightly floured work surface, roll both pieces of dough into 25cm rounds and use one to line the prepared pie dish. Lie the other piece of dough between 2 sheets of greaseproof paper and refrigerate both until cold.

3. To prepare the apples, heat a large, heavy pan over medium heat. Add the butter and melt, then add the cinnamon sticks and cloves, and sauté for a few minutes until the kitchen is filled with the aroma.

4. Toss in the apple chunks and sugar, and cook uncovered for about 15-20 minutes until it forms a smooth, fairly dry compote. Allow to cool (you can speed this up by spreading it out on a baking tray).

5. Dollop the cold compote into the chilled pie case, discarding the cinnamon splinters. Brush the edges of the pastry with cold water—this will help the lid to stick.

APPLE PIE

6. Place the other pastry piece on top of the apples and press the edges together firmly to seal—either with your fingers or the back of a fork. Brush the top of the pie with the egg white and sprinkle with caster sugar. Use a sharp knife to cut several slits in the top to allow steam to escape.

7. Bake the pie for 40 minutes or until golden brown (cover with foil if it looks like it is browning too quickly). When done, remove from the oven and serve warm with lightly whipped cream, custard (see page 144) or ice cream (see page 168).

OTHER WAYS WITH APPLE PIES

All sorts of fruit can be added to an apple pie, depending on what's in season, in your garden, freezer or fridge. You need 1kg of filling for the pie above—try mixing apples with a few chopped stalks of rhubarb, some quince, plums, apricot, peach, pear, blueberries, raspberries or blackberries (any berries should be added to the cooked apple compote, otherwise they'll turn to complete mush). You can even mix in a number of apple varieties—think Granny Smith, Red Delicious, Pink Lady and Royal Gala, all of which have different textures and flavours. Granny Smith, Braeburn and Jonagold are all particularly good for pies, having a firm texture and crisp tart flavour.

BAD APPLE PIE

Shop-bought pastry will do at a pinch, but is nowhere near as flaky and buttery as homemade shortcrust. You might also find that if you neglect to put slits in the lid of the pie that it cracks open as it cooks.

Make sure to taste the fruit mix too, as some apples are sweeter than others, for example Fuji and Pink Lady. You can always up the amount of sugar as you go, but there's nothing you can do if you add too much at the beginning.

You also need to make sure you have just the right amount of filling—1kg of fruit is about right, but the quantity you end up with will depend on how long you cook the compote. You need just enough filling to give the pie a rounded crown—too little and the lid will sink, too much and you risk a messy pie explosion.

FRUIT CRUMBLE

Is there any dessert that smacks of mum's home cooking more than the humble fruit crumble? Hot, sweet and incredibly comforting, it can be made from just about any fruit, or combination of fruit, in season—apple, rhubarb, peach, apricot, berries and quince. And that's just for starters. The only other ingredients—at least in the traditional version—are flour, sugar and butter, roughly mixed together to resemble breadcrumbs.

The trick to getting the right calibre of crumb on your crumble is to keep it rough and ready. Whiz it hard in a food processor and you'll get something resembling fine sand. Crush by hand, or with a few short sharp pulses, and you'll get the desired crumbly pebble effect.

It helps to make sure that the butter is ice-cold (so it doesn't simply melt into the flour) and that the sugar is not too fine. Brown sugar is great, but demerara sugar is even better as it gives the crumble just that little bit of extra crunch. What you're aiming for is a golden crust, sometimes stained by eruptions of fruit juice from below, but never soft and cake-like or resembling porridge.

SERVES 4

Ingredients

900g fresh fruit (stoned and cored as necessary, and cut into chunks), leave raw except for the apple, which should be softened slightly in a pan with a little water and sugar

2 tablespoons caster sugar, or to taste, for the fruit

1 cup self-raising flour

½ cup demerara or brown sugar

125g butter, ice-cold, diced

Method

1. Preheat the oven to 200°C (400°F). Prepare the fruit and place in a lightly greased, shallow baking dish. Sprinkle with the caster sugar (the amount of sugar you'll need is dependent on the sweetness and ripeness of the fruit you choose to use).

2. For the crumble, combine the flour and demerara or brown sugar in a large bowl. Tip in the diced butter and rub with your fingertips until the mixture resembles large breadcrumbs, with a few larger pebbles thrown in for good measure.

3. Sprinkle with a few drops of cold water and rake through the mixture with a fork, until you have a lovely mess of crumbs.

4. Arrange the crumble roughly over the fruit, but do not press down. Bake in the oven for about an hour until golden and bubbling.

5. Serve hot with thick cream, custard or good-quality ice cream.

FRUIT CRUMBLE

A SHORT HISTORY OF CRUMBLE

Funnily enough for such a simple dessert, the crumble is a relatively recent invention, first turning up in American cookery books in the 1920s (under the name Apple Crisp).

Other close relatives of the crumble include Apple Brown Betty (which consists of layers of fruit and crumbs, served with a sauce), Eve's Pudding (slices or chunks of apple covered with sponge cake mix) and Apple Cobbler, where the fruit is covered with a layer of batter, pastry crust or biscuit dough instead of the crumble mixture.

In America, at least, this last variation goes under a number of aliases, including Apple Slump, Apple Grunt and Apple Pandowdy, which practically begs to be chowed down to a Dolly Parton soundtrack.

BAD FRUIT CRUMBLE

Crumble is named that way for a reason—the topping should just crumble away in your mouth. For that reason alone, I say no to many of the variations that modern cooks seem so keen to add. Cardamom seeds, for example, have their place in the kitchen, but certainly not in my crumble. The same goes for nuts, rolled oats or, worst of all, muesli. We're talking pudding here, not a colon-cleansing breakfast (although it has to be said that cold crumble spooned straight from the fridge makes a perfectly adequate snack at any time).

Bad crumble is also a result of poorly balanced quantities of crumble and fruit. You shouldn't need a jack hammer or spade to reach the fruit beneath—nor should the crumble be so finely spread that it gets swamped by the hot, fruity juices as they bubble away.

DESSERTS AND BAKING

PEACH MELBA

There's a good reason why retro cooking is cool again—in our hunger for the latest foodie fad, we nearly forgot the pleasures of brilliant ingredients, treated simply and with respect.

Take peach melba, for example. This classic dish of poached pears with ice cream has been around since 1892, when famed French chef Auguste Escoffier (1846-1935) created it for the Australian opera singer, Dame Nellie Melba, after she performed in Wagner's opera *Lohengrin* at London's Covent Garden.

As served to Dame Nellie, the dish consisted of poached peaches served on ice cream, in a dish set on a swan carved out of ice. Unless you're handy with a chainsaw and have ready access to industrial quantities of ice, we suggest you serve it more simply—as Escoffier later did at the Ritz-Carlton Hotel in London—minus the swan but with a sweetly tangy raspberry sauce.

SERVES 8

Ingredients

For the peaches

4 cups water

3 cups sugar

2 tablespoons lemon juice

1 vanilla pod, split lengthways

8 peaches, halved and stones removed

For the raspberry sauce

3 cups raspberries

¼ cup icing sugar

1 tablespoon lemon juice

To serve

vanilla ice cream (see page 168)

fresh raspberries

Method

1. Put the water, sugar, lemon juice and vanilla pod into a deep, wide saucepan and heat gently until the sugar dissolves. Bring the pan to the boil and let it bubble away for about 5 minutes, until it becomes syrupy, then turn the heat down to a simmer.

2. Add the peach halves in a single layer, pop a lid on the pot and poach the peaches for 3 minutes.

3. Using tongs or a slotted spoon, gently turn all the peaches over, cover again, and continue poaching for another 3 minutes.

4. Test the cut side with a sharp knife to see if they are soft—how long the peaches take to cook will depend on the ripeness of the fruit.

5. Once cooked, refrigerate the peaches overnight in the syrup—the pigment in the skins will colour the flesh of the peach as it cools.

6. In the morning, remove the skin of the peaches by rubbing gently. Discard the skins and return the peaches to the syrup.

7. Meanwhile, to make the raspberry sauce, liquidise the raspberries, icing sugar and lemon juice in a blender or a food processor.

8. Sieve to remove the seeds from the sauce and taste, adding more sugar if you need it. Pour the sauce into a jug and refrigerate.

9. To assemble the dessert, allow 2 peach halves per person and sit them in a pretty glass dish (ideally frosted) alongside a scoop or 2 of ice cream. Spoon the raspberry sauce over each and strew the lot with a few fresh raspberries.

FIRST PICK YOUR PEACH

There are hundreds of varieties of peaches but most fall into one of two categories. Yellow-fleshed peaches tend to be more acidic and tangy, while white-fleshed peaches are generally sweeter and lower in acidity.

Similarly, peaches can be either freestone or clingstone. As their names imply, freestone peaches have stones or pits that can be easily pulled away from the flesh, while clingstone peach literally cling on for dear life.

Make things easier for yourself and go for a freestone variety when making peach melba.

How do you know when you've got a perfectly ripe peach? The skin of yellow-fleshed varieties ripens to an orange tint, while the skin of white-fleshed varieties changes from greenish to yellow-white. They should also have just a little 'give' when gently pressed and smell sweet.

BAD PEACH MELBA

Like most dishes, peach melba can be ruined by the use of substandard ingredients. Tinned peaches, for example, nasty raspberry sauce from a bottle, or cheap supermarket ice cream that's basically a confection of chemicals, held together by ice crystals. Instead, go for perfectly ripe peaches (see above), ripened on the tree and handled with care thereafter, raspberries at their peak, and some homemade vanilla ice cream (see page 168).

Presentation is important for this dish too. I'm a big fan of delicate glass dishes that let you see the dessert from all angles. The different components are very pretty, when done well, so it seems a shame to hide them in a chunky china dish that only allows you to see the top.

SCONES

The first recorded mention of the term scones was in 1513. Its origin is thought to come from the Middle Dutch word *schoonbrood* (fine white bread), although others claim it comes from the Gaelic *sgonn*, meaning a shapeless mass or large mouthful, which is what my first attempts certainly were. Today, scones are variously known as rock cakes, fat rascals and singing hinnies, depending on where in the UK you might be.

Early scones were unleavened—with no baking powder to help them rise—and about the diameter of your head, but their evolution into something that sits more easily on a pretty side plate is probably the reason for their continued popularity at morning and afternoon teas around the world. There are just a few simple secrets to creating the lightest, fluffiest scones:

* Ensuring the butter and milk are at room temperature before you start baking will result in lighter scones and a finer texture. It's also easier to rub warm butter into the flour.
* Don't over mix the dough, and certainly don't knead it as you would bread dough, or the gluten in the flour will start developing and it'll become tough and heavy.
* For perfectly shaped scones, use a pastry cutter dipped in flour to cut scones from the dough. Be careful not to twist the cutter as you pull it off or the scones will rise unevenly. Use a straight up-and-down motion instead.
* Arrange the scones almost touching each other, but not jammed together, on a lined baking tray. As the scones cook, their sides will stay straight and even rather than sprawling all over the place.
* To tell if the scones are cooked, tap the top of one with your fingertips—it should sound hollow. Or you can poke a skewer into a test scone—if it comes out clean, they're ready.
* Wrapping the scones in a clean tea towel after baking will give them a soft crust.

MAKES 12 SCONES

Ingredients

3 cups self-raising flour, plus extra for sprinkling

1 tablespoon caster sugar

80g butter, cubed, at room temperature

1 cup full-cream milk, at room temperature

butter or jam (see page 142) and whipped or clotted cream, to serve

Method

1. Preheat oven to 220°C (425°F) and line a baking tray with baking paper.
2. Combine the flour and sugar in a large bowl. Rub the butter in with your fingertips until the mixture resembles fine breadcrumbs.
3. Tip in all of the milk at once and use a knife to mix it in roughly, then bring it together in a glorious soft ball with your hands. If the dough is a little dry and crumbly, just add more milk until it all comes together.

4. Turn the ball of dough onto a lightly floured surface and press and turn it over about 3 or 4 times until the dough is just smooth. Think of it as a hot potato—you don't want to touch it too much, or for too long!

5. Flatten the dough out with the palm of your hand until it's about 2cm thick. Then dip a 5cm-round pastry cutter in flour and cut out your first scone. Re-dip the cutter before each one.

6. Bring any scraps together into a new ball, press out again and cut more scones. These will be slightly less fluffy than the first batch, and are likely to rise less evenly.

7. As you cut out the scones, place them closely together on a baking tray. Sprinkle with extra flour and bake in the preheated oven for 10-12 minutes, until golden and cooked through.

8. Remove from the oven and immediately wrap them in a clean tea towel. Serve warm with butter, jam (see page 142) and whipped or clotted cream.

SUPERSTAR SCONES

Here are ways to transform a perfect but plain scone into a scone with a difference.

Cheesy scones: Leave out the sugar and add ½ cup grated cheddar and ½ teaspoon cayenne pepper to the flour mixture before adding the milk. Sprinkle the scones with extra cheese instead of flour before baking.

Herb scones: Add 2 tablespoons chopped fresh parsley, 2 tablespoons chopped fresh chives and 4 finely chopped spring onions to the mixture before adding the milk.

Wholemeal scones: Replace 1 cup of the self-raising flour with the same quantity of wholemeal self-raising flour, and add an extra splash of milk.

Brown sugar buttermilk scones: Replace the caster sugar with brown sugar and replace the milk with buttermilk. Sprinkle scones with brown sugar instead of flour before baking.

Spiced sultana scones: Add 1½ teaspoons mixed spice to the flour mixture before rubbing in the butter. Add ½ cup sultanas to the flour mixture before adding the milk. Sprinkle the scones with a little sugar instead of flour before baking.

Note: The two savoury versions can also be plopped on top of a slow-cooked casserole for the last 15 minutes of cooking time to create gorgeous savoury dumplings that soak up the rich juices. Make sure you leave the dish uncovered so that the dough rises and browns.

BAD SCONES

A final word of warning: should your attention stray and your scones singe, do not bother attempting to rescue them. Scraping the charred bits from the top disfigures them and will not remove that nasty charcoal taint.

BERRY TART

Nothing says summer more than a luscious tart layered with colourful berries at their peak. This dish brings together two key recipes—for sweet shortcrust pastry (see page 148) and a thickened pastry cream (see Vanilla Pastry Cream), which is essentially an extra-thick custard.

The whole dish is a doddle to throw together once these are made. In order to stop the pastry crust soaking up too much liquid, you need to bake it ahead of time and make sure it is perfectly cool before spreading with the custard mix. Painting a thin layer of redcurrant glaze over the crust before piling in the pastry cream also helps stop it going soggy over time.

Of course, fruit is the hero ingredient here, so make sure to choose the prettiest, tastiest specimens you can find. They can either be arranged in formal concentric circles or rows, or randomly scattered with a lavish hand.

Berries are traditional, but kiwi, pineapple, melon, peaches, plums, nectarines and mango slices also work well. To give the fruit a beautiful shine, as you see in cafes and restaurants, simply glaze the fruit with a little redcurrant jelly, thinned with a squirt of lemon juice.

If using paler fruits, such as kiwi, it's best to use a less reddish jelly. The glaze also helps stop the fruit from drying out and looking dull.

SERVE 6

Ingredients

1 quantity sweet shortcrust pastry, chilled (see page 148)

½ cup redcurrant jelly

2 tablespoons lemon or lime juice

2 cups vanilla pastry cream (see 165)

2 punnets mixed berries (raspberries, strawberries, blueberries, and so on)

Method

To make the crust

1. Preheat oven to 200°C (400°C) and lightly grease a 23cm fluted tart pan with a removable bottom. Evenly pat the chilled pastry onto the bottom and up the sides of the pan. Cover with clingfilm and place in the freezer for about 15 minutes.

2. With a fork, lightly prick the bottom of the pastry crust all over. This stops the dough from puffing up as it bakes. (Or cover the base with greaseproof paper, half filling with dried beans or rice—a technique known as blind baking).

3. Place the tart pan on a large baking tray and bake the crust for 5 minutes. Reduce oven temperature to 180°C (350°F) and continue to bake for about 15 minutes, or until the crust is dry and lightly golden.

4. Remove from the oven and place on a wire rack to cool completely before filling. The crust can be covered and stored for a few days.

To assemble the tart

1. Remove the tart from the pan. Warm the jelly and lemon juice together, and paint a very thin layer over the bottom and sides of the baked tart shell to prevent the crust from getting soggy. Let the glaze dry (about 20 minutes), then spread the pastry cream onto the bottom of the tart shell.
2. Arrange the fruit on the cream, starting at the outside edge. Rewarm the glaze and gently brush a light coat on the fruit.
3. You will need to refrigerate the tart if not using immediately, but make sure to bring it back to room temperature before serving.

VANILLA PASTRY CREAM

To make the vanilla pastry cream, make the custard (see page 144) but add 2 tablespoons extra cornflour plus 2 tablespoons plain flour with the egg yolks, before adding the sugar and hot milk.

Once thick enough to coat the back of a spoon, pour into a clean bowl and cover the surface with clingfilm to prevent a skin forming.

Cool the cream to room temperature and, if not using straight away, refrigerate until needed. It will keep well for up to three days, but make sure to give it a good beating before using to get rid of any lumps that may have formed. Vanilla pastry cream can also be used to fill profiteroles, éclairs, croissants, mille-feuilles and even cakes.

BAD BERRY TART

The joy of a fruit tart lies in the contrast between the crisp buttery pastry, the smooth pastry cream and the tang of the fruit. So, taking a mouthful and discovering that somehow all three have melded into a soggy mass is always disappointing. To avoid this happening, it's important that the pastry is cooked to a golden biscuity finish. Underdone pastry tastes of flour and is irredeemably stodgy. You should also assemble the tart at the last possible minute—the longer it sits around, the greater the chance that the liquid from the fruit and pastry cream will ooze into the base. Like most tarts, this one is best eaten on the day it is assembled.

To avoid your pastry shell crumbling as you remove it from the fluted pan, place your hand under the pan, touching only the removable bottom section. Slowly push the tart straight up, away from the sides. The fluted tart ring will fall away and slide down your arm, while you're left holding the tart triumphantly aloft. The last step is to remove the tart from the pan bottom—simply run a thin knife or metal spatula between the crust and metal bottom, then slide the tart onto your serving platter.

BISCUITS

Honestly, this recipe is so straightforward that a child of four could make it, assuming they can reach the food processor. You can also whip up a batch in the time it takes to walk to the shops for a packet of cookies, so why wouldn't you make your own?

Best of all, the biscuit dough can be stored in the refrigerator for up to two weeks, so you can slice off a chunk and bake as many biscuits as you like, when you like. The dough can also be frozen, well-wrapped, for several months, which is probably best for those who can't resist raw biscuit dough and would be tempted by its presence in the fridge.

The secret to the perfectly shaped biscuit is to chill the dough well before baking it. This not only makes it easier to cut the dough into discs, but ensures that the biscuits don't spread out too much as they bake.

MAKES ROUGHLY 48, DEPENDING ON HOW THICK YOU CUT THE ROUNDS

Ingredients

185g butter

1 cup brown sugar, firmly packed

1 free-range egg

1 teaspoon vanilla extract

2¼ cups plain flour

½ teaspoon salt

½ teaspoon baking powder

egg white, for brushing (optional)

caster sugar, for sprinkling (optional)

Method

1. Cream the butter and brown sugar together until fluffy. Add the egg and vanilla extract, and beat well.

2. Sift the flour with salt and baking powder. Stir into the creamed butter mixture, until the dough is smooth and well combined.

3. Shape the dough into long rolls about 5cm in diameter. Wrap these tightly in foil and chill in the refrigerator for at least an hour.

4. When you're feeling peckish for hot-baked biscuits fresh from the oven, preheat the oven to 180°C (350°F) and line 2 baking trays with baking paper.

5. Slice the refrigerated dough into thin discs and place them slightly apart on the baking tray. If desired, you can brush the tops with egg white and sprinkle with caster sugar.

6. Bake in a moderate oven for 7-10 minutes or until golden brown. Cool the biscuits on the trays and then store in an airtight container for handy snacking.

MORE BAKING FOR YOUR BUCK

For chocolate fiends, all you have to do is add 170g of good-quality chocolate chips (at least 70% cocoa solids) or chopped dark chocolate to the mix before baking.

Or for an assortment that will please everyone, divide up the dough into five portions—keep one plain and flavour the others as follows:

- *Coffee*: Add 2 teaspoons of instant coffee granules along with the flour.
- *Coconut and lemon*: Add ⅓ cup desiccated coconut and ½ teaspoon lemon essence.
- *Ginger*: Add 1 teaspoon of ground ginger.
- *Chocolate*: Add ½ tablespoon cocoa and ½ teaspoon cinnamon, and top with a chocolate button or almond flakes, if so desired.

Looking for a savoury biscuit recipe? Look no further. These cheese biscuits are all about the sharp tang of a good-quality parmesan, and the short, soft mouthfeel of butter cooked with flour. You can also use a good cheddar or hard goat's cheese at a pinch.

In a food processor, mix together 125g of butter, 250g flour, 80g parmesan, 1 egg and a pinch of salt. Pulse until they are blended together and the dough forms a ball. If this doesn't look like it's going to happen, add a few drops of water until the dough catches.

Remove the dough ball from the processor, shape into a sausage about 2cm in diameter, wrap in clingfilm and rest in the fridge for at least an hour. You can also freeze the wrapped sausage like this, and simply pull out from the freezer when unexpected guests turn up.

Preheat the oven to 180°C (350°F). Cut the sausage into coins 3-4mm thick and place on a greased baking tray. Cook for 10-12 minutes until golden. Cool, then serve as a snack. This recipe makes 30-40 biscuits.

BAD BISCUITS

While some might claim that there's no such thing as a bad biscuit, I beg to differ. The overly sweet ones that you get in a packet are the perfect example, with their slightly soft, sandy texture and uniform shape.

Great biscuits are a doddle to make at home, and if you make the time to chill the dough before cutting it, your biscuits will maintain their shape. Biscuit cutters and stamps can be employed if you're wedded to the idea of perfection, but I think the uneven variety look extra-homemade.

You also need to be careful with how thickly you slice the dough and how closely you place the biscuits together—too thick and too close and you'll end up with a solid tray of cooked biscuits, rather than separate discs. But if this happens, don't despair, they still can have a very important place in your kitchen. Just pop the stuck-together biscuits in a plastic bag, take out your frustration on it with a rolling pin, and voila! Ready-made crumbs for topping or mixing into some lovely homemade ice cream (see page 168) for your very own version of cookies and cream—you can say you planned it that way all along.

ICE CREAM

Since the dawn of time, well at least since Nero's time in Rome, frozen desserts have been considered a treat. Legend has it that Nero would dispatch his slaves into the mountains to retrieve snow, whereupon they'd rush back to the capital where the snow was mixed with nectar, fruit pulp and honey to create a dish that was fit for an emperor.

It wasn't until the 17th century that those without slaves were able to enjoy similar frozen treats, thanks to the discovery that mixing salt and ice or snow resulted in rapid cooling. Today, with refrigeration and electric ice cream churns, there's really no excuse for not making it yourself—particularly when it tastes as good as this.

The master recipe here is for a rich vanilla ice cream, but you can transform it into whatever flavour you desire by the addition of chocolate chunks, nuts, berry or mango purées, fudgy sauces, crumbled biscuits or meringue, or even lemon curd.

For a wickedly tasty chocolate ice cream, simply reduce the sugar to ½ cup, leave out 1 vanilla bean, and add 200g of best-quality milk or dark chocolate once the custard is thick enough to coat the back of a spoon.

MAKES 750ML

Ingredients

300ml thickened cream

300ml full-cream milk

2 vanilla pods, split lengthways

5 large free-range egg yolks

¾ cup caster sugar

sprinkle of salt

Method

1. Pour the cream and milk into a heavy-based saucepan. Scrape the fine seeds from the vanilla beans into the liquid, then toss the pods in as well. Heat for 4-5 minutes until almost, but not quite, boiling, then remove from the heat and leave to infuse for 15 minutes or so. Discard any skin that has formed on the surface and then remove the vanilla pods.

2. Place the yolks, sugar and a pinch of salt in a bowl. Using electric beaters, whisk for about 3 minutes until the sugar has dissolved and the mix is light, white and forms a ribbon.

3. Pour a little of the flavoured warm milk into the egg mix, whisking well, then pour the egg mixture back into the rest of the vanilla-flavoured milk.

4. Cook, stirring constantly with a wooden spoon, for 10 minutes or until the mix noticeably thickens and you have a custard thick enough to coat the back of the spoon. (When you draw your finger across the spoon, you should end up with 2 clear lines.)

5. Once the custard reaches this stage, stop it cooking further by pouring the mix through a fine sieve into a cold bowl, whisking like mad as you go. Allow the mix to cool, then refrigerate until very cold—at least 2 hours.

6. Pour mixture into a shallow container and freeze for 2 hours or until starting to freeze around the edges. Remove and whisk furiously. Return to container and refreeze. Repeat 2 or 3 times. Alternatively, churn in an ice cream machine to manufacturer's instructions until thick but soft enough to spoon into a container.

7. Transfer to a plastic container with a lid and freeze for at least 3 hours or until firm enough to scoop.

WORLD'S WORST ICE CREAM FLAVOURS

Experimentation is all very well in its place, but whoever came up with these ice cream flavourings should be banned from the kitchen. The following list was meticulously researched by doing a Google search for 'world's worst ice cream'. And yes, these are real products, sold in real shops or served by real chefs, to people who really should know better:

- Ox-tongue
- Tomato
- Fish
- Wasabi ginger
- Miso
- Squid ink
- Fried eggplant

For those at home who are tempted to experiment with new flavours and combinations, there are a few simple rules to follow—particularly if you are in the kitchen with a bunch of enthusiastic under-fives. Most importantly, no livestock—worms, snails or guinea pigs are unlikely to appreciate a spin in the ice cream maker.

Second, think about what flavour combinations you like before you sully your hard-prepared vanilla base with something that you'd never choose to eat if you were out at a restaurant. Sardines and jam, for example. If you wouldn't eat the ingredient by itself, or even in combination with something you love, don't expect it to miraculously work as an ice cream.

BAD ICE CREAM

Some may argue that any ice cream is good ice cream, but once you've experienced the joy of the real thing, made from a cooked custard that's rich in the best cream and eggs and real vanilla, you'll find it nigh on impossible to go back to the mass-produced stuff.

The only real way you can stuff it up is to skip or cut short the churning process, which will result in nasty little ice crystals rather than a smooth and uniform cream that melts easily in the mouth.

BROWNIES

The beauty of the perfect brownie is that it's both deliciously rich and surprisingly light, which allows you to eat many more than is strictly sensible before the inevitable chocolate-induced nausea sets in. Funnily enough, however, the very first recipe for brownies (from Fannie Farmer's *Boston Cooking-School Cook Book* of 1896) contained no chocolate, just molasses and nuts. It wasn't until the 1906 edition that the brownies we know and love today were born. The debate still continues as to what constitutes the perfect brownie—should it be crumbly and cake-like, or dense and fudgy? And fierce arguments rage over whether it should have a crust or no crust. The difference lies in the ratio of flour to other ingredients. More flour gives a less gooey brownie, different chocolates will give different flavours, and dark muscovado sugar (or brown sugar) will help highlight the fudgy taste. For brownies, it's important to have all the ingredients at room temperature before you start. Cold eggs and butter do not make for good baking. Beating the ingredients furiously after adding the eggs is another secret brownie fans swear by—but only if you want a thin, crispy, meringue-like crust. You can get the same effect by raising the temperature to 180°C (350°F) and cutting the cooking time to 20 minutes.

You should be very careful not to cook the mix for too long. Warm, barely set mud is what you're after. Once out of the oven, some swear by popping the whole tray into a roasting dish of ice-cold water to stop the mixture from cooking further.

MAKES 1 x 23CM TRAY

Ingredients

250g 70% cocoa solids chocolate

250g butter, preferably unsalted

300g caster sugar

3 free-range eggs, plus 1 extra egg yolk, lightly beaten

60g plain flour

½ teaspoon baking powder

salt

60g good quality cocoa powder

100g walnuts (optional)

Method

1. Preheat the oven to 180°C (350°F) and line a 23cm-square baking tin with baking paper.

2. Set a bowl over a pot of simmering water and add 200g of the chocolate, broken into pieces. Allow the chocolate to melt, stirring occasionally, and then immediately remove from the heat. You can also do this step in the microwave—cook on medium-high for 10 seconds, stir and repeat until melted.

3. Meanwhile, beat the butter and sugar together until light and fluffy, and break the rest of the chocolate into chips.

4. With the mixer still running, gradually add the eggs, beating well between each addition. Continue mixing on a high speed for 5 minutes until you have a silky consistency and the mixture has increased in volume.

BROWNIES

5. Remove the bowl and gently fold in the melted chocolate and chocolate chips, followed by the flour, baking powder, salt, cocoa and nuts, if using.

6. Pour your brownie mixture into the tray and bake. Test with a skewer after 25 minutes; it should come out sticky, but not clagged with raw mixture. If it does, put it back into the oven for another 3 minutes, then test again.

7. When ready, remove the tray from the oven and allow to cool for at least an hour before cutting into chunky squares and storing in an airtight container.

FOUR WAYS TO TURN BROWNIES INTO PUDDING

Icing your brownies with a couple of layers of different flavoured icings is one of the easiest ways to turn them into spectacular individual desserts.

Caramel and coffee, or coconut and raspberry icing—simply mix and match to create your own masterpiece. Layer with lightly cooked meringue, mousse, jelly studded with fresh raspberries, crème fraîche mixed with orange zest, or even a crunchy nut mixture. You can also create a scrumptious brownie stack, perhaps with bananas and cream in the middle.

Freeze brownies for a fabulous base for a frozen dessert. Mint ice cream works perfectly as a topping, as does a decadent caramel or chocolate sauce.

Skewer small squares of brownie with everything from marshmallows to fresh fruit to squares of vanilla sponge for a delicious dessert that's as fun to assemble as it is to eat. Drizzle with melted chocolate or serve with a sweet dipping sauce, such as fresh strawberry.

BAD BROWNIES

Brownies from a packet? No thank you. Likewise, brownies without the best chocolate you can lay your hands on are bound to disappoint. Of course, today, there is a bewildering array of chocolate choices: unsweetened, semisweet, bittersweet, sweet chocolate, different percentage cocoa solids, dark, milk, organic, fair trade and all the rest. Go for the darkest and highest percentage of cocoa solids you can find, I reckon.

And be aware that if you're tempted to try another recipe that's lighter on chocolate but heavier in the cocoa powder department, you'll end up with a softer brownie but with a crunchier crust.

CUPCAKES

Biscuits, slices and cakes are always tempting, but nothing signals a party more than a perfectly iced, teeny-weeny cupcake. You can cook these in muffin pans, but traditionally they're baked in paper cases, which make it a doddle to remove them from the pan and cuts down on the messiness factor when serving.

For the best results, preheat the oven and have all the ingredients at room temperature before you start cooking, as this makes them easier to combine and reduces the risk of lumps. Sifting the flour and sugar will also help prevent an uneven batter from spoiling an otherwise delectable little cake.

You need to be very accurate with the measurements: this is not the time to go freehand, as a little bit too much flour or not enough milk can upset the delicate balance required for perfectly light, fluffy cupcakes.

MAKES 30

Ingredients

2 cups self-raising flour

¾ cup caster sugar

125g butter, softened

3 free-range eggs

½ cup full-cream milk

½ teaspoon vanilla essence

For the icing

¾ cup icing sugar

2-3 drops food colouring (or 1 teaspoon cocoa)

1 tablespoon butter, softened

a little hot water

Method

1. Preheat oven to 180°C (350°F). Set out 30 paper cupcake cases.

2. Put the flour and sugar in a bowl, then add the butter, eggs, milk and vanilla essence. Beat hard until the mix is very smooth, then fill the cases until three-quarters full.

3. Bake for 15 minutes or until golden, test for doneness (a skewer will come out clean) then remove and cool on a wire rack.

4. For the icing, simply beat together the icing ingredients until smooth, then use to decorate the cupcakes. Either swirl the top of each cake in the icing, apply with a knife, or use an icing bag and decorative nozzle. All sorts of toppings can then be added—sprinkles, edible flowers, grated chocolate, marzipan shapes—the choice is yours.

POSH CUPCAKES

Whether it's due to a growing sense of nostalgia, or a nation falling for the fabulous creations that come out of New York's Magnolia Bakery—made famous by Carrie et al in *Sex and the City*, but cupcakes are very much in vogue. The more colourful the better—think delicately flavoured light sponge cakes covered in pink icing and cute, often sparkly, decorations.

To transform plain cupcakes into something special, mix fresh raspberries with fresh double cream in a bowl, using a fork to break up the raspberries as you go. Take a dozen cupcakes, slice a lid off the top of each one, place a dollop of raspberry cream inside and replace the lid.

You can also cut the lid into two and turn them into pretty angel wings. The cakes can then be drizzled with a little pink icing or dusted with icing sugar—perfect for a birthday party or dainty afternoon tea.

Add an element of surprise by using a squeezy bottle to inject a filling: flavoured custard, jam, chocolate sauce or creams of any variety.

And then there is the flavour of the sponge itself—banana, orange, chocolate, coconut, ginger and lemon, mocha, pomegranate, butterscotch, almond... You can either blend in some fruit or another ingredient such as desiccated coconut or almond meal, or simply substitute some of the liquid in the basic recipe for another such as orange juice, or perhaps strong coffee. You can ring the changes simply by flavouring the icing with something different. For example, pair a coffee cupcake with Kahlua-flavoured icing, banana cupcake with lemon and coconut icing, or a strawberry cupcake with a cream-cheese frosting.

BAD CUPCAKES

You can always tell an amateur batch of cupcakes by the way some are slightly larger than others. To achieve regularity in sizing, don't just pour the batter into the cases willy-nilly, but measure out equal amounts. An ice cream scoop works perfectly here, or simply fill a small measuring jug to the same level each time.

Wonky sizing sorted, you also want to prevent your cupcakes rising unevenly, which can happen if the paper cases are free to spread out as the batter bakes. Popping the paper cases into a muffin tray with similar sized holes is the best way to make sure you don't end up with some seriously strange-shaped cakes.

Many a batch of cupcakes has been ruined when an overly eager chef tries icing them while they're still warm. For the best results, make sure they are completely cool. You can even make them a day ahead and store in an airtight container, but again make sure they are cold before you store them, otherwise they'll sweat. Lastly, if you're using a creamy filling or covering with a whipped cream topping, keep them in the fridge to ensure you don't run the risk of food poisoning.

MERINGUES

Light as a puff of air—albeit with a few more calories—meringues are the perfect way to use up leftover egg whites from mayonnaise (see page 140) or custard (see page 144). Freeze the whites in lots of two and you'll always have the makings of a great dessert at hand. As an added bonus, freezing egg whites dries them out and breaks down the protein, so that the whites inflate even more.

The other tip to getting your meringues as light as clouds is to start with a scrupulously clean bowl. Don't use plastic, as the egg whites will not stiffen properly. The slightest blob of egg yolk, drop of oil or shard of shell can also prevent the whites from whisking successfully.

MAKES 16

Ingredients

2 free-range egg whites, whisked to soft peaks in a non-plastic bowl

5 tablespoons caster sugar

Variation
Add 2 teaspoons coffee powder or a few drops food colouring with the sugar

Method

1. Preheat oven to 120°C (250°F). Cover a large baking tray with non-stick baking paper, or use a silicone baking tray. Any oil is a no-no, as the meringues will soak it up like tiny sponges.

2. Add the sugar, a little at a time, to the beaten egg whites until the mixture stands in firm peaks.

3. Add the remaining caster sugar and continue to whisk until the mixture is very stiff and has a silky texture. Using a piping bag or a dessertspoon, carefully dollop 16 meringues on the prepared tray. You can also trace shapes, such as hearts or stars, on the baking paper and fill in the outline with the meringue mix.

4. Bake for 1-1½ hours or until they are crisp and dry, but not browned. The meringues should lift very easily from the tray when done to perfection.

5. Cool on a wire rack and store in an airtight tin. Serve plain or sandwiched together in pairs with whipped cream.

USES FOR MERINGUES

Meringues are brilliant on their own, but they also make a fine addition to other desserts. Eton Mess, for example, is basically a concoction of strawberries, crushed meringues and cream. This naughty but ever-so-nice dessert is traditionally served at Eton College's annual cricket match against the students of Winchester College. Depending on what's available, substitute the strawberries with raspberries, blackberries or even a sliced banana, squirted with lemon juice to stop it browning. You can also use meringues as 'angel wings' for desserts such as chocolate mousse, or folded through a fruit purée for a bit of crunch and sweetness. Poke shards into a top-notch ice cream (see page 168), or try simply dipping the bottom of the meringues in different kinds of chocolate and serving as *petit fours*.

BAD MERINGUES

Instead of being sugary pillows, meringues can sometimes deflate into sugary crumbs. Generally, this happens if the oven is too hot. Meringues need a long, slow cook—if the oven is too hot your meringues will get so light they'll disappear in a puff of sugar. Essentially, you want to dehydrate the egg and sugar mix, not bake it, so pop the tray on a middle or bottom rung, and let them cook slowly and surely.

Meringues can also fail if the egg whites have been beaten too hard. Too much beating causes the stiff egg whites to deflate; once this happens, there's nothing you can do but chuck the mix out and start again. Don't try making meringues from a pavlova recipe, although many of the same tips do apply. Proper pavlova (see page 176) also incorporates cornflour, or cream of tartar, and vinegar or lemon juice, which helps to achieve the crunchy outer shell and marshmallow-like centre.

PAVLOVA

This billowing cloud of sugar and egg white is the perfect finish to a family meal or a celebratory feast, but there are four key tricks you need to remember.

First, use very fresh eggs. These will be easier to separate, their proteins will be more stable, and they'll whip much better than those that are old or just out of the fridge.

Second, make sure the sugar is completely dissolved in the egg white. Check by rubbing some of the mix between your fingers. If it still feels grainy, keep whisking until it is completely smooth. Don't be tempted to miss out on adding the acidulant (such as lemon juice or vinegar) as this stabilises the egg whites and will help prevent your pavlova from cracking.

Third, think about how you like your pavlova. For a softer crust and a more marshmallow-like texture, cook it at a slightly lower temperature, say 140°C (275°F)—cooking at 150°C (300°F) will give a slightly crunchier crust and drier filling.

Finally, once the cooking time is over, simply turn off the oven and leave the pavlova in the oven until completely cool. Don't even open the door and take a peek as the change in temperature might cause your meringue masterpiece to collapse.

Once you have your perfect pavlova, you can decorate it with whatever fruit or other toppings take your fancy. Some prefer sweetened cream and strawberries, while others opt for crème fraîche, honey and mango, or a few sliced bananas tossed in lemon juice and raspberries for a colour contrast.

SERVES 8-10

Ingredients

4 free-range egg whites

pinch of salt

250g caster sugar

2 teaspoons cornflour

1 teaspoon white wine vinegar or lemon juice

2-3 drops vanilla essence

300ml cream (or a mix of cream and crème fraîche)

fruit (strawberry, passionfruit, raspberry, blueberry, kiwi fruit)

Method

1. Preheat oven to 180°C (350°F) and line a baking sheet with baking paper. Draw a 20cm circle on the paper as a guide.

2. Beat the (room temperature) egg whites and salt in a clean, non-plastic bowl until smooth, shiny peaks form.

3. Beat in the caster sugar, a little at a time, until the mix is stiff, shiny and light as air.

4. Sprinkle in the cornflour, white wine vinegar or lemon juice and vanilla essence, and fold lightly together. Dollop the mixture onto the prepared baking paper circle and smooth the top and sides.

5. Place the pavlova in the oven and immediately reduce the temperature to 150°C (300°F), or 140°C (275°F) for a softer outside and chewier centre.

6. Bake for 60-75 minutes (depending on your oven) then turn the oven off and leave the pavlova to cool.

7. When completely cool, top with fruit, cream, crème fraîche—whatever you choose.

8. You can also cook the pavlova several days in advance and store it in a cool, dry place in an airtight container.

THE DESSERT WARS

The jury is still out on whether the pavlova actually originated in New Zealand or Australia, but it's generally agreed that the inspiration for this delicious dessert was the Russian ballerina, Anna Pavlova, following one of her tours to the Antipodes during the 1920s.

One possibility touted by pavlova sleuths (and a hypothesis that allows both countries to hold their heads high) is that the original recipe came from the Australian writer, Emily Futter, in a 1926 New Zealand-published book, *Home Cookery for New Zealand*.

BAD PAVLOVA

Shop-bought pavlovas, while convenient, are packed with enough sugar to make your teeth ache and are often so dry that every skerrick of saliva will instantly flee your mouth. There's simply no comparison with the homemade variety, although many people are too nervous to chance their luck—perhaps because they are scared of the dessert's tricky reputation.

To ease your mind, here's how people generally go wrong:

* The egg whites won't whip up properly—this could be due to a dirty bowl or whisk, flecks of yolk or shell in among the whites, forgetting the acidulant or cornflour, or adding the sugar in one great rush at the start (this can double the time it takes to whip the whites to a foam).
* Sugary droplets on the surface of the meringue—overcooking.
* Liquid oozing from the meringue—undercooking.
* A golden suntan—oven temperature is too high.
* Total collapse—overbeating the eggs, or opening the oven door during the cooking or cooling time.

CHOCOLATE FUDGE CAKE

If you're going to blow your diet on a slice of chocolate cake, it makes sense to do it on something that is lusciously sinful all the way through. That means loads of eggs, loads of butter and sugar, and the very best dark chocolate you can get your hands on.

This simple cake is easy to throw together and is deliciously fudgy rather than spongy.

It is great with a cup of tea for elevenses, or as an afternoon pick-me-up, and you can also serve it as a dessert, perhaps with fresh berries or a raspberry sauce (like the sauce for peach melba on page 160) and a good dollop of whipped cream or ice cream (see page 168). It's very rich, so a little will go a long way.

MAKES 1 X 15CM CAKE

Ingredients

125g dark chocolate—the more cocoa solids the better

90g unsalted butter, softened

2 tablespoons flour

125g caster sugar

5 eggs, separated

Method

1. Preheat the oven to 180°C (350°F) and lightly grease a small 15cm cake tin.

2. Melt the chocolate in the microwave on medium-high stirring every 10 seconds, then mix it with the softened butter, flour, sugar and beaten egg yolks.

3. Beat the egg whites to very stiff peaks in a scrupulously clean bowl. With a gentle lifting motion, taking care not to squish all the air out, fold the egg whites into the chocolate mix.

4. Bake in the oven for 35 minutes, until a thin crust appears on the top of the cake. Poke it with a skewer—unlike more traditional sponge cakes, the centre will seem somewhat uncooked, which is exactly the effect you are after.

5. Remove the cake from the oven and allow to cool slightly in the tin. Once cool enough to handle, remove from the tin and allow to cool completely on a cake rack.

CHOCOLATE FUDGE CAKE

THE ICING ON TOP

You can cover the top of the cake with lightly whipped cream and fresh berries if you like, or you can go the whole hog and ice it properly. The best chocolate icing uses real chocolate, with not a sprinkle of cocoa powder in sight.

Simply combine 200g of good-quality chocolate and ½ cup thickened cream in a bowl and microwave on medium-high for 1 or 2 minutes, stirring every 30 seconds, until almost melted. Stir until smooth. Set aside for about 30 minutes to thicken up, then ice your cake.

You can make it even fancier, even more chocolatey, by decorating with large curls of chocolate. To make these, simply run a clean potato peeler down the edge of a block of chocolate, letting the curls drop to a plate below. These are very delicate, so handle them carefully.

BAD CHOCOLATE FUDGE CAKE

Doesn't exist. Somehow, even the driest, crumbliest chocolate cake will disappear within minutes, particularly if you serve it with lashings of cream or ice cream. To avoid the curse of a too-dry cake, make sure you remove it from the oven before the centre is completely cooked. When you insert a skewer, it should come out coated with cake batter, rather than completely dry and clean. The top should be cooked to a crust—the centre moist and fudgy. Should the opposite result occur, and your cake is simply too gooey to slice evenly, just call it chocolate pudding, and serve with a spoon.

That said, there's nothing more disappointing than salivating over a beautifully decorated chocolate cake only to find that under its blanket of icing and artful decorations is a flavourless cake that's distinctly lacking in chocolate. This will happen in you use bad-quality chocolate and/or overcook the batter. You should also make sure that the batter is well mixed as it more than a little disconcerting to bite into a moist, dark slice only to find a pocket of powdery white flour. You have been warned.

BREAD

Nothing tastes better than a thick slice of freshly baked bread, still warm from the oven, with a generous spread of butter. And making it is possibly one of the homeliest, most satisfying things you can do—particularly if it's cold and rainy outside and you're planning on snuggling up with the newspaper or a good book.

The joy of bread-making is that between a couple of bursts of activity, there's not much for you to do except catch up on your reading. And while you're doing that, the yeast will be doing all the hard work. Once it's introduced to the flour and warmed, it starts giving off carbon dioxide, which gets trapped in the dough as tiny air bubbles that make the bread rise and give it its texture.

Salt is also added to give flavour, but there's lots of other things you can add too (see Taste Sensations). Of course, practically every culture around the world has its own variation of this staple—think *chapatis* in India, pita in the Middle East, *focaccia* in Italy and *injera* in Ethiopia, to name but a few—but right here, right now, it's time for a crusty white loaf…

MAKES 1 LOAF

Ingredients

melted butter, for greasing and brushing

500g white bread flour, plus extra for kneading

7g (1 sachet) dried yeast

1 teaspoon salt

1½ cups tepid water

extra water, for brushing

oil or butter, for greasing

Method

1. Lightly oil a 10 x 20cm loaf pan with some of the melted butter.

2. Tip the flour, yeast and salt into your very largest mixing bowl and tumble it round with your hands to combine. Pour in almost all of the water and mix it to a sticky dough with a wooden spoon. Add a little more flour until you have a dough that's soft, springy and only slightly tacky to the touch.

3. Turn the dough onto a surface liberally sprinkled with flour and knead for 8-10 minutes or until smooth and elastic. There's no great secret to the technique—just use the heel of your hand to push the dough away from you and then lift the upper edge back towards you and work it back into the dough. Press your finger into the surface of the dough—if it springs back, it has been kneaded enough.

4. Give the bowl a swipe with oil or butter, then pop the ball of dough in and roll it over, so the surface is lightly coated. This helps stop the surface of the dough drying out, which can slow down the rising process. Cover with a damp tea towel and then place it in a warm, draught-free place.

BREAD

5. Leave the dough until it has doubled in size, then tip it out onto the floured surface and knock it around a bit until it reduces to its original size (this gets rid of excess carbon dioxide that can give the loaf a too-strong yeasty flavour).

6. Preheat the oven to 200°C (400°F). Shape the dough into a loaf-shape and pop it in in the pre-prepared loaf tin. Brush lightly with the melted butter.

7. Leave the loaf tin in a warm, draught-free place, as before, for about 30 minutes or until the dough has risen about 1cm about the top of the tin.

8. Gently brush the loaf with a little water. Bake for 30 minutes or until golden and cooked through. The best way to tell when the loaf of bread is cooked is to tap it on the base with your knuckle. If it sounds hollow—kind of like a drum—it's cooked.

9. Right now, you need to turn the loaf onto a wire rack and let it cool. If you leave it in the tin it will start sweating and the crust will get soggy, which is definitely not what you are after.

10. Once cool, store the loaf in a well-ventilated place at room temperature. This bread is best eaten on the day it is made. However, it makes great toast 1-2 days later. Make any stale leftovers into breadcrumbs and freeze in a sealed freezer bag.

TASTE SENSATIONS

* *Herb bread:* Add ¾ cup chopped fresh herbs (parsley, chives, oregano, basil) to the dry ingredients before adding the water. Great with cream cheese.
* *Sweet fruit and walnut bread:* Replace 300g of the plain flour with wholemeal flour. Add 2 tablespoons brown sugar, 2 tablespoons ground cinnamon and 1 teaspoon mixed spice to the dry ingredients before adding the water.
* Knead 200g of mixed fruit or raisins and 150g chopped walnuts into the dough after kneading for the first time and before proving.

BAD BREAD

There are a couple of things to keep in mind. First, the water needs to be lukewarm to activate the yeast. If the water is too hot, it can kill the yeast. Too cold, and nothing will happen. Kneading is important. This process distributes the yeast evenly through the dough and strengthens the gluten in the flour. If you don't knead the dough enough, the bread will be crumbly in texture.

You can also stuff up a perfectly good loaf by rushing the rising process, or putting it somewhere too hot, which will kill the yeast and make the dough useless. The slower the rising, the heavier and denser the bread texture will be. But don't overdo it: if left to rise too long, the bread will be uneven and have large holes.

DRINKS

HOT CHOCOLATE 184
SMOOTHIE 186
LEMONADE 188
ICED TEA 190
CHAMPAGNE PUNCH 192

CHAPTER 11

DRINKS

Since the first life forms crawled out of the primordial slime, most have relied upon water to remain hydrated. Nowadays humans have a million other options at hand, some of which are infinitely more pleasurable than others.

Here are just five drinks—both hot and cold—readily available at your local bar or café, but nowhere near as good as the real thing, made from scratch by your own fair hands.

HOT CHOCOLATE

Sometime in the late 1500s, this drink took Europe by storm, but long before then, as far back as 1500-400BC, the ancient people of Central America had discovered that grinding up the seeds of the Theobroma cacao tree and mixing them with water made for a fabulously tasty beverage.

This recipe is simple enough to make any time you're looking for a chocolate fix, but it does depend on having some good-quality chocolate at hand. Most of the better varieties list the percentage of cacao that they contain on the label (the more the better) and these will deliver a richer more chocolatey taste than those bars where a tiny amount of chocolate is basically used as a colourant.

You should also use full-cream milk—never soy—or even a mixture of milk and pouring cream, if you're going to be really decadent.

In which case, you may as well go the whole hog and add a slosh of a liqueur, such as cognac.

For those who prefer their hot chocolate frothy, more like a latte than a flat white, you can first froth the milk using a stick blender or milk steamer, then stir in the chocolate until melted. Or you can use the blender attachment on your food processor—just make sure to hold the lid down tightly so you don't get splattered with hot milk.

But the indulgence doesn't end here, once you have poured your perfectly made hot chocolate into your favourite mug, cup or bowl (as is the accepted way in France), you can liberally sprinkle it with marshmallows, chocolate curls and cocoa powder, or add a splash of whipped cream. Afterall, if you are going to have a calorie-fest, you might as well really push the boat out.

SERVES 4

Ingredients

1 litre full-cream milk

400g good-quality dark chocolate, finely chopped

½ teaspoon ground cinnamon

pinch of salt

whipped cream, to serve (optional)

marshmallows, to serve (optional)

chocolate curls, or good-quality cocoa powder, to dust

Method

1. To make the hot chocolate, place the milk in a medium saucepan over medium-high heat and bring to a simmer. Whisk in the chocolate until melted and then whisk in cinnamon and salt. Do not allow to boil!

2. Serve hot, perhaps with a dollop of whipped cream or some marshmallows, and sprinkle with chocolate curls or cocoa powder.

CHILLI HOT CHOCOLATE

Now you may think that combining chilli and chocolate is a modern-day fusion trick, but in fact the Aztecs were the first to think of it, about a millennium or so ago. And it's brilliant.

Simply add a fresh red chilli, split lengthways with the seeds removed, to the milk as it's warming. Remove the chilli before serving, and sprinkle ground chilli powder on top to serve.

Other possible variations include peppermint hot chocolate (just add a dash of peppermint essence or use peppermint chocolate), vanilla, mocha (add a splash of very strong black coffee and a few drops of vanilla essence) or even white chocolate. Which isn't chocolate at all, but does contain cocoa butter…

BAD HOT CHOCOLATE

Never confuse hot chocolate with hot cocoa—hot chocolate is made by melting real chocolate into milk, while hot cocoa mixes milk with cocoa powder—essentially, chocolate that's been pressed free of cocoa butter fat (the good stuff), meaning it will lack a lip-smacking richness.

Hot chocolate is also full of milk proteins, which is why, if you're not careful, a nasty skin may form on the surface of your drink. This is caused by the proteins clumping together as they heat up—denaturising, as the scientists would say. To minimise the effect, don't let the milk boil and whisk or stir constantly as it is warming through.

You won't get a scab on top of your hot chocolate if you use skim milk, as this has had the fat removed so the protein has nothing to bind with, but the richness will be missing—and isn't that the point? Better to learn how to make it properly in the first place.

SMOOTHIE

As well as being fast to whip up, smoothies have the added benefit of being a great way of hiding stuff that's good for you, but not that interesting—like fibre, vitamins and your daily ration of fruit. Perfect for kids and wimpy grown-ups, and equally good served at breakfast, for a snack or even a late-night dessert.

A good smoothie will be smooth (duh), ice-cold and packed full of fruit. Some insist on adding weird stuff, like spinach, celery or even parsley, and while it may look wonderfully green and healthy, somehow it's nowhere near as appealing to actually drink.

Ice is a key ingredient, making your smoothie taste extra refreshing and giving it a better texture. You can also freeze chunks of fruit or berries and use in place of ice cubes to chill the drink, and this way you get double the amount of fruity goodness.

Make sure you leave the motor running long enough for the liquid to be whizzing around and the solid contents liquefied. The liquid at the top should be swirling and circulating back down to the bottom. It can take up to 45 seconds for this to happen depending on the power of your motor and how full the blender attachment is.

SERVES 4

Ingredients

3 ripe bananas

1 cup fresh or frozen strawberries, plus extra for serving

1⅓ cup natural yoghurt

1 cup full-cream milk

2 tablespoons honey

1 cup ice cubes (you can leave this out if your fruit is already frozen)

Method

1. Place all the ingredients—fruit, yoghurt, milk, honey and ice cubes, if using—in a blender and blend until smooth.

2. Pour into chilled glasses and serve immediately.

OPTIONAL EXTRAS

Why stop at bananas and strawberries? Have fun experimenting with whatever you have to hand (within reason). To get you started, here is a selection of superstar smoothie ingredients:

* Peanut butter or protein powder—for extra protein, of course.
* Wheat germ—as a source of complex carbohydrates, soluble fibre and those all-important B vitamins.
* LSA mix—ground linseed, soy and almond meal—for extra fibre and essential fatty acids.
* Cocoa powder, which partners beautifully with bananas and adds a touch of indulgence to the brilliant post-sport, early-morning pick-me-up.
* Using skim or soy milk instead of regular full-cream milk will help reduce the fat content of an otherwise healthy beverage.
* For a thicker drink, replace the natural yoghurt with frozen yoghurt or ice cream.
* For a little metabolism 'kick', add a slight pinch of ginger (ideally freshly grated) to your mix. Bear in mind that ginger will spice this up a bit so go easy at first.
* Fresh mint leaves (or even mint ice cream) add a refreshing tingle to a berry or watermelon-based smoothie, making it perfect for summer sipping.

BAD SMOOTHIE

It's all in the name: smoothies are meant to be smooth, and not surprise you with chunks of partially chopped fruit. Likewise, smoothies are considered to be a healthy option—not a calorie-laden diet bomb. Too many commercial smoothies rely upon sugar and lots of fruit juice for taste and volume, but are short on the good (and more expensive) stuff, like real berries.

Beware of smoothies that have been left sitting around for too long. This causes the ingredients to separate so your smoothie becomes more of a chunkie. Smoothies are always best made and consumed fresh.

That said, it is possible to make smoothies ahead of time and freeze them (for up to three days). Just blend your smoothie, pour it into a freezer-proof glass or container with an airtight lid, and store in the freezer until needed. Once partially thawed, give it a good shake or stir to get it back together again and drink immediately—this makes for a great breakfast or lunch on the run.

LEMONADE

Lemonade is dead easy to make, right? Just squeeze some lemons and add some sugar and water. But how to make lemonade so that it tastes perfect every time?

Get the proportions right—essentially 1 cup sugar, 1 cup water, 1 cup lemon juice. This ratio makes a fairly sweet lemonade, so reduce the sugar content to ¾ cup if you don't have a sweet tooth, or if you are using a sweeter lemon variety, such as Meyer.

The other secret to perfect lemonade is to start by making a sugar syrup. By dissolving the sugar in the hot water, you end up with a smooth syrup, rather than having the granular sugar sink to the bottom. Cooking the syrup with the lemon rind adds a depth of lemony flavour that you won't get from juice alone, but make sure to peel it very thinly, avoiding the white pith, as this will add a bitter tang.

SERVES 6

Ingredients

1 cup sugar (can reduce to ¾ cup)

thinly pared rind of 3 lemons —use a potato peeler

1 cup water (for the sugar syrup)

1 cup lemon juice

3 to 4 cups ice-cold water (to dilute)

Method

1. Make the sugar syrup by heating the sugar, lemon rind and water in a small saucepan until the sugar is dissolved completely. Allow to cool, then strain.

2. When the syrup is cool, combine with the lemon juice.

3. Taste and adjust to suit your personal preferences, remembering that it will be diluted with water.

4. When ready to serve, simply mix with the ice-cold water, to your desired strength.

5. Serve with ice and very thinly sliced lemons. The lemonade will also keep well in the fridge for up to a week.

MINTY REFRESHMENT

Everywhere you go in Israel, particularly in the summer, you'll see people slurping down vivid green drinks that look like rocket fuel.

Known as *limonana*, the name comes from the Hebrew and Arabic words for lemon and mint: *limon* and *nana*. And that's pretty much what the drink is made of: lemon and mint, plus heaps of ice, all whizzed to a slush in a blender. Perfect for hot summer days, and even better with a slug of vodka added to it.

To make 1 litre of *limonana*, simply combine 3 cups of ice with a 1 cup of homemade lemonade (see recipe opposite), and 1 cup of mint or spearmint leaves, removed from their stalks (save a few to garnish).

Place all the ingredients in a blender and whiz until smooth. Serve immediately, garnished with the mint leaves.

BAD LEMONADE

Proportion is everything when it comes to lemonade. You don't want it to be mouth-puckeringly sour, nor do you want it too sweet. Taste it and adjust until it suits your personal preference—either way the recipe opposite is far, far more delicious than the stuff you buy that's packed full of artificial colourings and flavourings.

The temperature at which you serve your lemonade will also have an effect on its final flavour, so make sure to taste after you've added the water. Lemonade is generally served icy cold for maximum refreshment—for some reason, it never tastes quite so good when served lukewarm. If adding ice to help chill the drink down, add it at the very last minute so that it doesn't have too much time to melt and dilute the drink beyond your desired proportions.

ICED TEA

Iced tea, a drink once only read about in American novels or heard on hillbilly TV shows, is now a staple in shops and cafés everywhere. And now that it's back in fashion, you'll be pleased to hear this deliciously refreshing beverage is dead easy to make at home, and a great alternative to fizzy soft drinks. Hell, you probably have everything you need to make it in your cupboards right now.

All it takes is a few tea bags, water and a bit of sugar and you are on your way. Just make sure to follow these simple rules:

★ The right tea—when drinks are served cold, the flavours can become dull. Use a more strongly flavoured tea, such a Lapsang Souchong or Darjeeling, for best results. You can use either traditional black tea or lighter-tasting green tea.

★ Don't let it brew too long—if you like your tea strong, use more tea bags rather than leaving the bags in to stew for longer. Letting the tea over-brew brings out the tannins and can make it taste bitter. For weaker tea, reduce the steeping time rather than taking away tea bags as this will give you a better flavour.

★ Use a sugar syrup, not plain sugar—granulated sugar will leave sugar grains in your glass.

★ Cool the tea before refrigerating—putting hot tea into a cold fridge will make it go cloudy, so allow it to cool completely before chilling in the fridge.

★ Keep it real—if flavouring with lemon, don't be tempted to use artificial juice from one of those horrible plastic lemons. Fresh squeezed lemon juice from fresh lemons gives the very best flavour.

MAKES 2 LITRES

Ingredients

5 teabags

8 cups boiling water

2 tablespoons sugar syrup, or to taste (made from boiling together 2 cups sugar and 2 cups water until the sugar is dissolved). This makes more than you need for this recipe, but it is handy to have in the fridge when the desire for iced tea strikes

fresh mint leaves, to garnish

Method

1. Make a brew of tea with the teabags and water. Allow the tea to brew for no more than 5 minutes, or it will taste bitter.

2. Pour your brewed tea into a large jug containing the sugar syrup mixture and stir. Adding the hot tea to the cold water helps prevent the finished drink from becoming cloudy.

3. Allow to cool then refrigerate until very cold.

4. Serve in glasses over ice, garnished with sprigs of mint.

ICED TEA

FLAVOURED TO A TEA

* For a tangy alternative, make a jug of plain iced tea as above, but add 60ml of lemon juice to the sugar syrup before you add the hot tea. Test for sweetness—the tartness of the lemon might demand a little more sugar.
* For peach iced tea, peel and slice 2 perfectly ripe peaches. Place in the boiling water at the same time you add the tea bags. You can remove before serving or not, as you wish.
* You can get the same kind of fruity flavour by using a fruit tea as the base: blackcurrant tea, pomegranate tea, raspberry tea, and so on. Or simply add a dash of apple juice and some very finely sliced apples.
* You can also throw in flavourings such as finely sliced ginger (deliciously refreshing), mint or even tamarind pods. Syrups and other liquids too make a fine addition: think rosewater, maple syrup, apricot nectar... the list is endless.
* To give your iced tea a bit more pizzazz, half-fill ice cube trays with water and freeze. Place some fruit (such as blueberries, raspberries or citrus slices) on top of the half cubes, top up with water and freeze again.

BAD ICED TEA

Bad tea leads to bad iced tea. So make sure you don't over-brew the tea, or squeeze the tea bags when removing them, as this will lead to a nasty bitter taste. You should also drink it when freshly made, as the flavour deteriorates the longer it is left sitting around.

CHAMPAGNE PUNCH

Parties have been going better with punch for hundreds of years now, thanks to an ancient East Indian recipe involving five key ingredients—alcohol, sugar, lemon, water and tea or spices. Incidentally, the word punch is derived from *panch*, the Hindi word for five.

British sailors of the 1700s were very fond of the stuff—doubtless for is effects—and its popularity spread quickly once they brought the recipe home to good old Blighty. Today, there are millions of recipes based around different core ingredients—rum, champagne, claret and so on—but to my mind, champagne is the one that shrieks *party*!

As it's a mixed drink, the quality of the alcohol isn't going to stand out, so go for a medium-quality brand, not your most expensive bubbles. Alternatively, there are many other options you can use instead of champagne—Spanish cava, Italian prosecco or any sparkling wine—the main thing is that it's cold and dry (and definitely not sweet).

Punches often involve pieces of chopped fruit making an appearance, but there's nothing worse than getting a mouthful of warm fruit in the middle of a cold drink. Make sure that this fruit is well chilled before adding it to the mix. Or freeze it completely, which will do away with the need for added ice, which will only dilute the drink's potency as it melts.

SERVES 8

Ingredients

3 cups chilled sparkling wine

3 cups chilled lemonade

⅔ cup chilled raspberry vodka

⅔ cup Cointreau

200g frozen raspberries

1 lime, thinly sliced

1 lemon, thinly sliced

ice cubes, to serve

Method

1. Combine the sparkling wine, lemonade, vodka, Cointreau and raspberries in a large jug.

2. Add the lime and lemon slices, tip in some ice cubes (or frozen fruit) and serve.

CHAMPAGNE PUNCH

PLANTER'S PUNCH

Planter's Punch is one of the most historical rum punches, the sun-drenched island of Barbados even has its own ditty to help anxious hosts remember the recipe: "One of Sour, Two of Sweet, Three of Strong, Four of Weak."

In other words, one part lime juice, two parts sweetener (generally some kind of juice), three parts alcohol (preferably local rum, in this case), and four parts soda water.

It's traditionally served with a dash or two of Angostura bitters and some fresh nutmeg sprinkled on top.

BAD PUNCH

Good punch should deliver a kick, but it shouldn't be a knockout blow. Of course, this might not be the host's fault, as guests—particularly teenage guests—are notorious for topping up the punch bowl with whatever alcohol is at hand. So what might start the night out as a simple rum punch may end the night as more of a champagne, beer, red wine, tequila slurry.
Keep it simple, and keep it topped up, lest your guests feel inspired to do it themselves.

This next point is also important if you want your punch to have real oomph. Half the fun of punch is in its sparkle, so make it just before you intend serving, lest your bubbles go flat. Proper glasses (champagne flutes) are an essential.

A final word of warning: use the biggest ice cubes or chunks you can possibly make or find. Smaller cubes melt faster, and will make your punch watery before it gets properly cold.

NOTES

NOTES

NOTES

NOTES

NOTES

NOTES

NOTES

ACKNOWLEDGEMENTS

As always, many thanks to Geoff Slattery, Helen Alexander, Olivia Hudson and the rest of the team at the Slattery Media Group for their boundless enthusiasm and killer eye for detail. And it would be plain wrong not to acknowledge the chefs, cooks and food writers and, more recently, bloggers who've shared their tips and tricks for perfection over the centuries. By passing on this kitchen lore, we all benefit.

Finally, a big thank you to my family and friends, who suffered through the trials and errors in my kitchen, and happily ate most of the results.

ABOUT THE AUTHOR

Victoria Heywood has written about food, travel, relationships and health for numerous magazines and newspapers, and is the author of 28 non-fiction books. She now lives in Melbourne with her son, one dog and two cats—none of them are likely to appear on the menu anytime soon. Her previous cookbooks with the Slattery Media Group are *Celebrate! with Food and Wine* and *Possum Pie, Beetroot Beer and Lamingtons*—a collection of Australian family recipes from 1868-1950.

ABOUT THE ILLUSTRATOR

Bill Wood has worked as a full-time illustrator for more than 20 years and likes to cook when he's away from the desk and computer. Working for clients all over the globe, he enjoys adding his own unique touch to every individual commission. Illustrating food has always been a speciality for Bill, who believes it has a lot in common with cooking—knowing when to have fun and be a little irreverent with the style, not take it too seriously and yet remain respectful to the subject matter at all times, and not to overcook things.